CHURCH PLANTER

FIELD MANUAL:

EXPLORING

◆————————◆

Dr. Tom Wood

This Material is produced by Church Planters for Church Planters

Contributors included:
Matt Adair, Christ Community, Athens
Scott Armstrong, City Church Eastside, Atlanta
Craig Brown, City Church of East Nashville, Nashville
Bob Cargo, Director Church Planting, Perimeter Church
Rod Entrekin, Christ Church, Suwanee
Alan Foster, East Lanier Community Church, Flowery Branch
Peter Harris, Camden Church, Camdentown/London
Nathan Lewis, Evergreen Presbyterian Church, Portland
Jim Moon Jr., Crosspoint Encuentro Church, Smyrna
Steve Resch, Walnut Creek Church, Columbus
John Smed, Prayer Current, Vancouver, BC
Shayne Wheeler, All Souls Church, Decatur
Jim Whittle, Equipping Leaders International, India Director

P.O. Box 3284 • Alpharetta, GA 30023

Thanks to:
Rev. Jim Moon Jr., colleague and friend
who edited each module for content.

Rev. Steve Resch, friend and fisherman extraordinaire,
who formatted the modules.

Ms. Lori Helm, who graciously copy edited and kindly offered much help.
J.S. Carter, writer and encourager. Glad you are in my life!

Dedication:
Dedicated to my mentor in Church Planter Assessment and Training,
Dr. J. Allen Thompson.

I am grateful you took me under your wing many years ago.
You had no idea what you were getting into! Your godly life and rich
wisdom has been an example to thousands of others.
The training modules are based on the ten dimensions in his Church
Planter research found in The Church Leader Inventory™.

Using this material

It has wisely been said that, "Necessity is the mother of invention." It was out of necessity for Church Planter training materials that were gospel-centered, Church Planter specific, and outcomes based—and that were done in a format that could be used on a monthly "in the trenches" type setting—that I developed these materials. Several Planters added their learning and experiences into each module.

There is some very fine weeklong Church Planter training available in the USA: Global Church Advancement (Orlando, FL), Exponential (Orlando, FL), and Dynamic Church Planter Institute, just to name a few. Various church tribes and networks host regional two or three day boot camps. Redeemer City to City (NYC) hosts Church Planter Incubator™ for their partners. Those are all solid training events. I recommend a Church Planter attend some form of formal training prior to planting a church. Just like coaching, it's a non-negotiable.

We found that what Planters need is training that happens in their monthly rhythm. Some educators call it "Just in Time Learning." Where do you best learn to plant a church? By attending a weeklong conference? Not really. You learn to plant a church while you are planting the church—so the best place to get trained is "on the job" or "on the field of play," as it were.

According to Dr. Ed Stetzer's research on healthy church planting, Church Planters who are involved in a peer-learning community that meets at least once a month increase their survivability by 135% (www.newchurches.com). The best place for the *Church Planter Field Manual* to be used is in a monthly Church Planter meeting that also incorporates other important factors like coaching, prayer and community.

Each module can be used by an individual Church Planter or with a coach, or in a leaderless learning group (the materials will lead the group) or with a facilitator/instructor. There are action points for outcome type thinking, activity and learning.

The Church Planter Field Manual was written with the contribution of several Church Planters for Church Planters. It is comprised of four books with five modules in each book.

1. **Exploring:** Networking and People Gathering; Preaching the Gospel in a Post-Everything world; Shepherding God's People; Time Management for the Planter; Missional Engagement Part 1.

2. **Climbing**: Building a Launch Team; Worship Design for the New Church; Handling Conflict in the Plant; Planting a Generous Church; Missional Engagement: Part 2.

3. **Fishing:** Disciple Making; Team Building for Beginners; Gospel Life of the Church Planter; Leadership Development; Planting a Reproducing Church.

4. **Resting**: Personal Prayer Life of the Planter; Building Gospel Community; Confessions of Old Church Planters; Reviewing and Renewing the Mission; Planter's Family Life.

Thanks for your interest in Church Planting.

CONTENTS

Networking & People Gathering

Chapter One

Unlocking the community and
gathering for mission

I. Networking—Meeting People and Developing Contacts in the Community

It's day one—the first day on the job as Mr. Church Planter. The books are all unpacked and the office is pretty much set up. The kids are in their schools. You know where the grocery store and the doctors are. You are now officially a new Church Planter in your community. Now what do you do? Be careful, what comes natural might take over if you are not intentional in this area. What you need to do is start Networking in the community and city.

A. Why Do I Network?

The Gospel is a mission. You are Gospel sent. Jesus has sent you to a city, a context, and a people. It's time to start meeting people and networking in the community. That is the activity, but what are some outcomes? There are more, but three outcomes are big:

1. Learning your community context.

"It's important to have a working knowledge of the people who live in your geographic market. This marketplace may range from an established, easily identifiable rural community to a complex melting pot of cultures residing in a rapidly changing metropolitan area" (George Barna, *The Power of Vision*).

Begin with a *missionary mindset*. You are living and learning **your mission field**.

You probably have collected all the demographic, socio-graphic and spiritual-graphic data prior to arriving. Now you are meeting the real people, asking questions, listening and learning— Attitudes, values, hurts, lifestyles, religious beliefs or lack thereof, etc.

"…we traveled to Philippi, a Roman colony…we stayed there several days. On the Sabbath we went outside the city gate to the river, where we expected to find a place of prayer. We sat down and began to speak to the women who had gathered there…" (Acts 16:11-3).

"Men of Athens! I see that in every way you are very religious. For as I walked around and looked carefully at your objects of worship I even found an altar with this inscription; To an Unknown God." (Acts 17:23).

As you learn your community by Networking, it will shape your preaching, evangelism, apologetics, and deeds of mercy, prayer life and your church's ethos. Basically, learning your community context will shape the way you do gospel ministry in your city.

From day one, the development of ministries and activities for the establishment of the church should be identified as "good for the community".

2. **Creating a pool of contacts.**

"Everyone I meet is a potential convert, attendee, member of the new work or someone who will help promote a positive view of the new church."

Your work Schedule should be anywhere from 2-4 hours per day networking in a 10 hour workday.

3. **Make yourself known as a friend of the community/city.**

People in your community will most likely be suspicious of you and your agenda. Be very careful to meet people and listen, lest you be seen as a user. You are an outsider, so be respectful of those who live and work there.

Have a Gospel answer to the question: "Why are you here?" or "What do you do?"

B. Networking is Highly Relational

Find the ways in your context in which lines of relationships are made. One Church Planter, who spent enormous amounts of time meeting with people in the community, was asked more than once, "Dave, are you running for mayor?"

In every community there are strategic people, "gatekeepers" or "tribal leaders". One Church Planter met the mayor, who then introduced him to several key business leaders in the community at Rotary Club.

LEADERSHIP TYPE NETWORKING

- Mayor, City Administrator
- Chief of Police
- Elementary, Middle, and High School principal, counselor, and your kids' teachers
- Local pastors, religious leaders—RC priests, Imams, Rabbi
- City council members
- Local charities, mercy type ministries

MARKETPLACE TYPE NETWORKING

- Chamber of Commerce
- Fire Chief, EMS drivers
- Developers
- Local Real Estate agents
- Manager of large grocery store
- Wal-Mart managers
- Bank managers
- Newspaper editors
- Mercy ministries in town

COMMUNITY NETWORKING

- Neighbors
- Neighborhood presidents
- Schools through your kids
- Athletics—sport teams (one CP bought a book on Soccer so he could coach)
- Coffee shops, pubs
- Bookstore clubs—(visit non-church/Christian groups)
- Churches—as you visit them (not sheep stealing)
- Hosting neighborhood block parties, Christmas parties
- Dance classes—usually people getting married soon

SOCIAL MEDIA NETWORKING

- Facebook, Twitter, or Linkedin (For an article on how to use Facebook, visit www.cmmnet.org)
- Blogging
- Website

C. Build Bridges to the Community

- o   Teach classes at public schools-substitute teach, offer parent workshops
- o   Volunteer at schools
- o   Coach little league
- o   Volunteer as Police Chaplain
- o   Join tennis/swim associations
- o   Parent Teacher Association
- o   Join a local gym/workout
- o   Host fun events
- o   Use the same dry cleaner, eat at same places, meet owners and servers
- o   Home Owners Association—join and lead the welcome or social committee
- o   Community service projects

In brief contacts with people, always show interest in them as a person and ask easy questions—"Can I ask you a quick question? If you were going to go to a new church what would you want it to be like?"

D. Build Along Relational Lines

The Gospel spreads primarily through relationships.

- o   Use referrals
- o   Have a tracking sheet or Customer Relationship Management tool (i.e. Outlook Express)
- o   If you want to make 600 contacts in 3 months, that is 10 people every day 5 days a week for 3 months

E. Suggestions on Making Contacts

Place a high value on Networking! People appreciate the person who destroys the social awkwardness of the initial meeting.

- Always be early, never late - it places high value on the person you are meeting.
- This is harder than writing a sermon
- You are responsible to make contacts, no one else
- You will get discouraged
- It is hard work
- Meet everyone you can
- This is not evangelism (though they may turn into contacts later).
- This is not core group recruiting (though you might get interest)
- Stick to the 'script' and purpose of your meeting—glean info on community and spotlight your new church's interest in the community. Do not get sidetracked into politics!
- Always ask for a referral. *"Is there someone else you think I should talk to?"*
- Ask them if they would like to be put on a mailing or email list to receive periodic updates on the new church
- Send a personal, hand written thank you note for their time and help. Tell them you will be back in touch later if that's ok.

"COLD CALLING" BY REFERRAL:

"Hi, I'm _____. Your friend _____ gave me your name and told me you would be a good person to talk to about our community. I am not selling anything. I am new to the community and am trying to meet with people like you who can help me learn about our community. I am starting a new church in this area and would like to ask you some questions about the area. Would you be willing to meet with me for about 30 minutes?"

FACE TO FACE:

"Thanks for taking time out of your schedule to meet with me. As I told you, I'm new to the area and plan to start a new church here that will serve the people, who live, work, and play here. To do that:

1. Tell me about our community. What do you like about it? What is it like? Needs? What do people do for fun, recreation? What do you see most people doing on Sundays?

2. What advice would you give me about starting a new church here? What would you suggest to a new church that you think would benefit our community? How would it improve the quality of life here?"

HOW TO FIND RECEPTIVE PEOPLE

You might consider becoming the community "hub". You can begin to connect people to one another as you meet others. Be a servant to the community leaders.

Consider creating a community website or Facebook account that connects all the contacts you have made together. Become a knowledgeable resource to the community. Help dispel the assumption that you are using the community to start a church rather than being a good neighbor and the church serving the community.

"Un-churched people are most responsive to a change in life-style during periods of transition…people in stable situations, with few complications or interruptions are not usually open to radical departure from their established life-styles" (Charles Arn).

↓ACTION ITEM: MAKING CONTACTS

Discuss with your coach (20 minutes).

Brainstorm with your coach about ways to begin your Networking. Be creative. Think outside box.

List the five prime "communities" in which to begin my Networking?

①

②

③

④

⑤

How many hours a week will I plan for this?

Who are some strategic leaders (gate keepers or tribal leaders) I need to meet?

Decide on some Outcomes:

I want to meet _____ people per week.

I will attend/create _____ bridge building communities.

I will collect _____ names of people to follow up with later.

II. PEOPLE GATHERING FOR THE NEW CHURCH

The shift from Networking (meeting with people and getting to know the community, the lifestyles, needs, and values in the community) to gathering people together can be a difficult transition for some.

It is impossible to overstate the high importance of the skill for the Church Planter in gathering new people. Even if the plant is a hive-off or daughter church, gathering new people is vital to the health and growth of the new church in reaching its community.

Some people are good at starting things. That ability is demonstrated by a trail of new activities or ministries that they leave behind them. Others are better at building on things that someone else has started. Those who have started things generally have learned how to gather new people and connect them with the new endeavor.

"Probably one of the most difficult aspects of church planting is simply gathering your first fifty people. (Second only, of course, to gathering your next fifty, and the fifty after that.) Not surprisingly, however, there are factors related to the life and growth of a church unique to the number of people attending" (Steve Nicholson & Jeff Bailey, *Coaching Church Planters*).

The Art of the Start: People Gathering

"There is no 'one' way to go about [gathering people]. Ministry and church planting is inescapably incarnational and contextual, and what works for you, your gifts, your team, your geographical area and your target group may well not work for another person. Try lots of things.

Know your culture well. Pray and listen to the Holy Spirit. Those are the most important things" (Steve Nicholson & Jeff Bailey, *Coaching Church Planters*).

The Gospel gives you permission to be creative in your cultural context, given your style and family stage. Gather <u>missional</u> Christians as well as the un-churched. Ask people from your previous church to move with you in the mission of planting the new work. Some may be willing to relocate. Gather people who can serve short-term as well as long-term. All paid staff should be people gathering as well.

1. What is Your Style?

"People go about the gathering process in different ways. Some people are good at one-on-one conversations; their gifts and attractiveness naturally come out in personal interactions. Others more naturally gather people with their up-front skills; interacting with large groups, communicating, teaching, and casting vision. However it is expressed, though, the ability to gather people is one of the first and most fundamental of abilities that must be present in the Church Planter" (*Kairos Church Planting Assessment*).

A. One-on-One Approach

If you are highly relational in your approach (High I or S) and have gifts of hospitality (shared with your spouse), this might work very well for you.

- Meet with people individually, in marketplace or homes, pubs. Have a business card with contact info on it.

- Share your story, but keep it simple. Ask them about their story and LISTEN WELL. Find commonality. Care for others and their lives.

- Invite people to your home or to some meal together at a "third" place. Two meals a week are at least ten contacts every week. Invite two people per meal and you will gather *twice as fast.*

"We're friends with people we do things with…We don't seek our friends…we associate with people who occupy the same small physical spaces we do" (Malcolm Gladwell, *The Tipping Point*).

B. Large Group Approach

If you tend to be more of a highly motivational upfront influencer with great communication skills (High D type), you might do better at gathering new people using your strengths in the larger setting. However, if you do not have a group to start with, you must rely on personal, high touch, type gatherings.

- Plan, host, and invite people to larger events—"True Brew," "Calvin and Hops," "Skeptics Forum"—in a neutral environment.

- Attend block parties, BBQ's, picnics, felt-need seminars. Ed Stetzer's research says that if a Planter hosts block parties, it increases the survivability of the plant by 230% (USA, Church Plant Survivability Study 2007, **www.newchurches.com**).

- Christianity Explored or special type studies; Bible studies on the Gospel for Christians.

Work to leverage your strengths in people skills. Consider your spouse and family's interests, gifts, and calling. Make people gathering a family affair. Your kids might be one of the best people meeting, people gathering means you will ever have.

For instance, one of my daughters is a "special needs" adult. She does not have any real sense of "boundaries" when she meets people (almost everyone is a friend). We met all sorts of people because of her friendliness and openness.

One of my Church Planter friends said, "The #1 gatherer for us is a 38 year old mentally challenged woman."

C. Utilize a Combination of Both One on One and Large Group

1. Pray for the "Connectors" you met while networking and gather them or help them gather with you.

"Connectors…know lots of people. They are the kinds of people who know everyone…Connectors are important for more than simply the number of people they know. Their importance is also a function of the kinds of people they know…They are people whom all of us can reach in only a few steps, because, for one reason or another, they manage to occupy many different worlds and subcultures and niches" (Malcolm Gladwell, *The Tipping Point*).

Who are the Connectors in your Network of contacts?

2. Ideas on gathering your first 50 people.

The following ideas are referenced from *Coaching Church Planters* by Steve Nicholson & Jeff Bailey:

o Seek a "Fishing License" from the mother church or sponsoring churches in the region to ask members of their churches to become 'missionaries' to your community. A Fishing license allows you to drop a line into their membership and take new mission minded Christians on your journey.

o Ask the Spirit to go out before you and open doors of opportunity with people. Ask Him to send you to people he has been preparing.

o You have to go out and get people. This is the most important thing. You can't wait for them to come to you— they won't. Your preaching, as good as it might be, is not going to be the gathering tool you think it might be.

o Do everything as humanly possible to make connections, re-connections with people you have networked, and build relationships with them. Be creative.

o Put all your time and energy into gathering people you have "Networked."

o To get to your first 50 people, you must prioritize your time almost exclusively on gathering. Plan for those meetings, large or small.

o Write down how many people you can meet in a week. Pray for contacts and for favor with them.

Once you have your first 50, you can cut your time in half. Use half of your time to care, teach, train some of them to gather and manage whom you have and the other half to go out and gather the next 50.

Remember, you are personally responsible to gather the first 50 people. When you get them, you are responsible for the next 50 people too!

The primary goal is building relationships with people—spending time together, laughing, enjoying life together, answering questions they may have, eating, playing games, going places together, etc. Do NOT use people to accomplish your goals!

3. Four questions people are sub-consciously asking as you interact with them.

- o ***Do I like him?*** Is he someone I can hang out with? Is he likeable? Do I like his family? Is he trustworthy?

- o ***Does he know where he is going?*** We used to say that you lead with vision. But not any longer. The first question is the personable one. But that doesn't mean people don't care about where you are going. They are. What is your vision for the future?

- o ***Does he have what it takes to get us there?*** This is an ability question. You may have great vision, but if they lack confidence in your leadership ability you will not have many followers.

○ *What does he want from me? What is my role?* After figuring out that they really like you, that you have a compelling vision for the future, and you probably have a good idea of how to pull it off, they will want to know what you want from them.

4. **Three keys to remember in gathering people.**

A. Prayer. You have been sent by the Lord, so be bold. Gospel prayer is effective to reach people. Be humble!

B. Story. You have a story. Get it down and make it compelling about how God is redeeming you.

C. Retention. Retain the right people. Do not try to gather all your contacts into your group. Some people don't need to be part of a new church start up.

●————————————●

Love Well, Risk Big,
Laugh a Lot, Work Hard,
Pray Harder, and Enjoy the Ride

●————————————●

↓ ACTION ITEM: GATHERING

Discuss with your coach (20 minutes).

What is my personal style strength? (1 = Poor, 5 = Excellent)

1. On scale of 1-5, how would I rate my one-on-one skill? Why?

2. On scale of 1-5, how would I rate my large group skill? Why?

3. What types of Gathering meetings, events or meal will I use that will best facilitate my personal skill?

4. What types of outreach will best communicate the beauty of Christ in the Gospel to this community and will set this church as a unique expression of that Gospel?

5. If you have others already in your core or staff, how will they best network and gather in the community?

Remember:

You are completely forgiven—you have nothing to hide.
  You are perfectly righteous in Jesus—you have nothing to prove.
    You are eternally loved—you have nothing to fear.
      Rely on the Holy Spirit to lead you and to provide for you!

Courage flows from the Gospel embraced!

Preaching the Gospel in Post-Everything World

Chapter Two

"I am not ashamed of the gospel for it is the power of God to save people…"
Apostle Paul in letter to Roman Christians.

INTRODUCTION:

Most Church Planters sense the call of God to preach. One of the reasons you probably went into the church planting business was so you could preach the gospel to others. You sense you are a good communicator, passionate about preaching, and confident that you can get others to hear you preach.

Preaching the gospel is a top priority for the church. Preaching the gospel, according to the Scriptures is the chief means (the way God employs to get grace to work in us) of grace in us. For instance, "Through the means of the soil, of rain and sunshine, God always and constantly causes the seed that is sown to sprout and to develop into the ripened ear and thus produces the crop, provides bread for man" (Herman Hoeksema). So preaching is the way grace is worked in us.

"Question 96 of Benjamin Keach's Baptist Catechism (Q. 89 in *The Westminster Shorter Catechism*): How is the Word made effectual to salvation? Answer 96: The Spirit of God maketh the reading, but especially the preaching of the Word, an effectual means of convincing and converting sinners, and of building them up in holiness and comfort through faith unto salvation.

It is interesting that the catechism places special emphasis on the formal preaching of the Word, which can only take place when the church is gathered together"(Luke Stamps, *Gospel Coalition* blog, "Especially Preaching").

3 Challenges Church Planting Preachers Commonly Face:

1. **Preaching week in and week out will be one of the most challenging pieces of church planting you will face.**

    You have all the built up zeal and passion to preach, and think you have loads of things to say that will help your congregation, but after the weekly grind of preaching, it might become a huge burden—especially if you have not preached on a weekly basis before.

2. **Most preaching you have heard—most evangelical preaching in the past 20 years—has been oddly enough, not gospel preaching. It has been largely "Moralistic Therapeutic Deism."**

    "[MTD] is based on a humanistic, man-centered way of seeing our problems. And it offers solutions that we can manage and accomplish in our own strength and wisdom…" (Thomas & Wood, *Gospel Coach*).

    The end result of this approach to preaching the Bible is that God is a god for your gaps. "You are basically a good person, with some flaws. Here are God's teachings on how to correct those flaws, and He will help you correct them, if you will just let go and let him help" or "Here are 5 tips on how to succeed in becoming the person God wants you to be—and you want to be all you can be, don't you?"

    You have grown up with that system of thought whether you are aware of it or not.

3. **"We are not in Kansas anymore."**

You are communicating to a mixture of post-modern, post-protestant, post-Catholic, post-Secular, post-everything culture. We are essentially post-everything. And it is in the cities and the suburbs. There no longer exists in our North American culture a Christian narrative. The Story is lost to our current generation. What is left of any semblance of Christianity is negative. "The vast majority of unchurched people think that Christians hate them" (Jerram Barrs, Covenant Seminary).

Consider the following presuppositions of the post-everything world:

- God is the same for everyone—He is the good in all that we see. No need for a personal relationship with God.

- You can be anything you want to be and accomplish anything, including perfectibility. Believe strongly in the human potential.

- All religions are basically the same. No one should be too strict in their religion, or think their religion is right and everyone else is wrong. Extremism is wrong; we must be tolerant of all.

- What you do and what works is what is right. Doesn't really matter what you believe as long as you are helping others.

- There is no objective standard of right and wrong that is right for everyone.

- You must be true to yourself if you are going to be happy…and being happy is the supreme value of them all.
- Popular Secularism has become the dominating culture. The Media (TV talk shows, Reality TV, Movies, and Hollywood lifestyles, etc.) and our "pop-culture" of ideas is a contradictory mix of modernity and post everything.

Your community, no matter if it's city or town or suburbia is a mix of post-everythings. This is wonderful news to the missionary Church Planter. It means we are similar to 1st century Church Planters, entering a multi-faith society, with no understanding of Christianity—there wasn't Christianity!

We have a unique opportunity in the history of the world to present to people a glorious, Loving Father who (though we despised his love to pursue our own loves and came under the curse of death) sent the "Son he loves" to become a substitute for us; that we might, by faith and repentance, become adopted sons and daughters, and enter into his renewing Kingdom. We are liberating slaves!

I love this quote: "I freed a thousand slaves. I could have freed a thousand more if only they knew they were slaves" (Harriet Tubman).

Before we dig in, let's take the challenge:

1. **Preaching is to have primacy in your ministry**.

   It is one of, if not the primary way people "get the Gospel" (Romans 10:14-15 and Titus 2:11-14). This means you need to work hard at learning your craft. Just as the pro-golfer Phil Mickelson has to work hard at golf—practice, coaching, watching film, etc.—you need to learn and work at it. It may be a gift you have, but you can improve. You can always improve.

2. **The Gospel must be primary in your preaching.**

There is a danger, even for you gospel cowboys, to end up preaching something else. It happened to the Apostle Peter, and it can happen to you. It will be easy to fall into preaching doctrine, or religious moralism, or even use the word "Gospel" in the message but never actually preach the "Gospel".

Some people love to hear their particular doctrines taught deeply. Some people, (maybe most people) love Moralistic Therapeutic religion because it gives them an element of control. "Give me the things I need to do (morality, behaviors, will) and God will make me happy."

3. **Preaching well takes work**.

You will not be preaching like Tim Keller, Matt Chandler, Andy Stanley, Steve Brown or Mark Driscoll in a few short weeks; nor should you ever try to be them. And, you don't need 10,000 hours of reps to be a good preacher. Malcolm Gladwell's study meant that to be a freakish expert at the craft those folks had spent over 10,000 hours at it. Nevertheless, your preaching, if you want to be a solid gospel communicator will take time, practice and experimentation.

Charles Spurgeon said, "If any man will preach as he should preach, his work will take more out of him than any other labor under heaven."

Your work must include doing proper exegesis of your audience. What are their suspicions about religion? Are they Skeptical about people with agendas? What dialogical questions are they asking as they listen to you preach? What things have wiped them out in life? What false saviors are they living for right now? You need to learn their stories of their creation, fall, redemption and renewal.

Preaching the gospel begins with you preaching the gospel to yourself. So we will spend time considering how you deal with the gospel yourself. In Psalm 51, the writer ends the famous passage with the words, "Then I will teach transgressors your ways and sinners will be converted."

Most preachers would agree that they want to teach people God's ways and see lost people get converted. So when, according to the Psalmist, will that happen?

I. Beginning with Your Own Heart

"Then I will teach transgressors your ways and sinners will be converted" **(Psalm 51:13).**

A. You Need the Brokenness of a Wrong Spirit

In verse 2, David begins with, *"My iniquity and my sin…"* and verse 3, *"For I know my transgressions."* He admits that he knows he broke God's Law or Moral will. David confesses that he is constantly aware of his sin. In verse 4, he acknowledges that his sin was against God alone. He is broken about his sin. He believed a lie that life could be found outside of God.

The evil one has whispered a lie into the Universe, and ever since our parents listened to it, we have too; "You cannot trust the heart of God. God is not for you. You must take life into your own hands. At the center or root of all our sin, is to doubt the goodwill of God: To not believe Him or His way" (Martin Luther).

Then David adds in verse 5, *"Surely I was sinful at birth"*. This goes even deeper than he thought. David said, "I naturally lean toward the forbidden, toward self fulfillment, self dependence—I am so selfish. How long have I had this tendency? Since before birth—I was conceived a sinner. I was born a sinner."

You are worse off than you ever dared to let anyone know—even yourself.

David is saying, your whole personhood is <u>more deeply infected</u> and corrupted by sin than you thought. He is saying, "Yesterday, I was living right and today, oh my, I have blood on my hands. Yesterday, I was doing all the right things, life was good, and then today, Wham, I'm ruined."

Steve Brown said, "You wouldn't be so surprised at your sin if you didn't have such a high view of yourself."

The fact that we are amazed at our fall, surprised at what you said or did this past week, really shows how much deeper your sin goes because it reveals that we are full of self-righteousness.

B. Seek the Renewal of a Right Spirit

"Create in me a pure heart, O God and renew a steadfast spirit within me" **(Psalm 51:10).**

Renew my inward spirit and make the cross so attractive to me. May The Greater beauty I seek be Christ. I need a higher affection. How will we resist temptation? Can you resist by sheer willpower or by just saying "No"? We must have God create in us a greater heart, on the inside, a heart power, a renewed will. As Jonathan Edwards said, "Our affections are not too strong, they are too weak!"

C. Find the Ministry of the Holy Spirit

"Do not cast me from your presence, or take your Holy Spirit from me" **(Psalm 51:11).**

His work is an inside job. Only the Holy Spirit can work on a person's heart; you can't get there with your own words. You can will yourself to change. God changes the inner being.

David is saying, "I know I have to have the ministry of the Holy Spirit working inside me." It is easy to clean up the outside and fake it and make others think that we are ok, but God is working in the heart. He is working on the inside.

Can we let our consciences be our guides? People in your churches think so. You hear it a lot. "I just felt" or some people say, "I know what the Bible says, BUT..."

Do we really believe that if we set up some rules that they will stop us from wandering away? Do you honestly believe that you can keep people your congregation pure by setting up accountability groups?

Remember in the story, David says to his aide, go find out who that woman is. He reports back, "She is Bathsheba the daughter of Eliam and the WIFE of Uriah, ah you know them, and she's married). That is an accountability partner and it didn't help keep David from his sin.

We can have the TRUE accountability partner at work in us, the Holy Spirit, stirring us up. His job is to point us to true beauty, the true desire of our hearts, souls, and delights; Jesus Christ.

D. Enjoy the Freedom of a Liberated Spirit

"Restore to me the joy of your salvation and grant to me a willing spirit..." **(Psalm 51:12b).**

Paul wrote it this way; *it is for freedom that Christ has set you free...use your freedom to serve one another in love.*

Are you experiencing an inner deep river of joy? You say, well I'm not sure…or rarely ever do I feel happy and joyful". This may be the issue—maybe not. But it is worthy of your inspection.

When you know God's rich forgiveness, and are personally repentant of your known sins, you should hear sounds of joy in the soul. Why? There is a deep relief. The music of joy causes me to dance. Why? God's pleasure is on me.

When I have the Brokenness of a wrong spirit and the Renewal of a right spirit and then the presence of His Holy Spirit—His fullness in my life, not that I lost the Holy Spirit—I am restored with the <u>joy</u> again of salvation. Not a restored salvation, but the joy of knowing His closeness. God really isn't mad at me!

Then, I will teach transgressors and sinners will be converted.

E. You Will then Have Gospel Influence on Others

You give others grace, not un-grace to the degree you have been given grace. Think of this! Think of it! When you come to God in repentance and find it fresh and free, you will offer it toward others, freely.

John Calvin, one of the great leaders of the Reformation wrote, "Those who have been mercifully recovered from the fall will feel inflamed by the common law of love to extend a helping hand to their brethren." Another commentator wrote, "The sinner who has experienced a sense of his own sin; the forgiveness of God and sweetness of restored joy will show concern for others."

So, the Gospel is for the unbeliever and the believer. "The Gospel is not just how we become Christians but how we grow as Christians. We do not preach the gospel for salvation and then biblical principles to live the Christian life" (Dick Kauffmann).

"The most desperate need of both unbelievers and believers each and every Sunday is to hear and appropriate the Gospel of Christ to their lives" (Jack Miller).

➥ ACTION ITEM: POINT ONE, YOUR OWN HEART

1. Think of 3-5 people who have been transformed in their lives by the application of the Gospel in your sermons.

2. What are some of the things that have changed in their lives?

3. Think of the people who have been converted by the Spirit through your preaching of the Gospel.

The following is adapted from Dr. Steve Childers:

Renewal of the church almost always begins with the personal renewal of the church leaders. The godly church leader is often called by God to be the congregation's "Chief Repenter" joining with the Apostle Paul who said, "I am the chief of sinners!" (1 Tim 1:15). Dare to pray the old revival prayer, "Lord, bring revival and let it begin with me."

1. If you feel there is little spiritual power in your life and ministry what do you suspect is going on inside you?
2. How is your form of Christianity truly supernatural? (Acts 1:8).
3. How is Christ dwelling in your heart by faith in your normal day-to-day affairs of life? (Eph 3:17). What is the present value of the Cross?
4. How are you truly abiding in Christ, experiencing a moment-by-moment, ongoing dependence on Christ as a way of life? (John 15).
5. How are you keeping in step and being filled with the Spirit, proceeding under the Spirit's control daily? (Gal 5:25, Eph 5:18).
6. Have you lowered the biblical standard of spiritual transformation and accepted as normative a level of experience that God does not mean for you to accept? (Gal 3:1-3).
7. What are the "idols of your heart"? What are you looking to for true happiness in life other than your relationship with God through Jesus Christ? Is it approval, comfort, security, etc?

II. Your "STYLE" in preaching

All leaders have a style. Typically that pastor/leader also communicates or preaches in that style. We are usually strong in one and have a secondary style. The strong style is the one we default to when we preach. Do you know "who" you are in your communication style? Are you aware of what style you have? Are you more of a prophet, king, or priest?

Are you someone who likes to tell the Truth—here it is, wrapped up nice? Are you so priestly, caring about the wounds, being tender, focused only on our adoption, to the neglect of the disciplines of grace? Do you like to give steps and have solid outlines or power points? Let's consider your style of preaching using the following descriptors so you can identify your own personal style.

A. Prophet, King, or Priest

1. The Prophet—LOGOS/WORD. Prophets are "Truth Tellers" and their focus is on knowledge. They might say, "This is what God says about…" or "I teach the Bible". The emphasis is on the words, exegesis, outlines, and doctrines. They love to confront false idols; confront religion, other "faiths" and wrong doctrines. They tell us God's will.

"A prophet…disrupts the paradigm of comfort and complacency. But when he shouts at me, he also invites me to desire and dream of redemption…A prophet exposes our subtle turn to indulgence and self-congratulation. He points out our self-righteousness and underscores the evidence that our current condition is not true, good or lovely" (Dan Allender, *Leading with a Limp*).

Key Operating Ideas for Prophets:

- Challenges the Status quo
- Confronts the 'world' and/or religion
- Disrupts people's ideas, presuppositions or world view
- Exposes and lays people bare
- Truth Tellers—"This is the way it is"

Dr. Tim Keller writes that the Prophet's role is: "To expound and teach the text so they understand Christ. The aim is to explain the text in its overall biblical context, which is always to ask, 'what does this tell me about the person/work/teaching of Jesus?'"

2. <u>King</u>—ETHOS. This is how God wants you to live. The focus is on what you are to do. The emphasis is on application, and the context/situational. Kings give systems and models for living the Christian life. They offer security for living by giving good outlines, charts, and lists.

Key Operating Ideas for Kings:

- Directions for life
- Outlines, points, sub-points, lists
- Loves Power Point presentations
- Offer security for living
- Directions for how to live life

Dr. Tim Keller writes that the King's role is: "To apply and counsel with the text so they put on Christ. The aim is to use the text on the hearers' practical life issues and problems, which is always to ask, 'how am I failing to rejoice in and live as if this were true about how Jesus is and what he did?'"

3. <u>Priest</u>—PATHOS. Their emphasis is on who you are. The focus is on the 'be' or the position. Priests are similar to counseling type issues, and typically preach in psychological terms. They are sympathetic to the hurting and the wounded. They understand the hurts and grief of others.

Key Operating Ideas for Priests:

- Comforts—offers peace, refuge
- Invites and welcomes
- Counselor
- Sympathetic to hurting

Dr. Tim Keller writes that the Priest's role is: "To adore and worship with the text so that they rejoice in Christ. The aim is to experience Christ through the text as you present it, so the hearers have a true sense of God on their hearts."

Jesus Christ assumed all three Old Testament offices of Prophet, Priest, and King, perfectly. We, of course, are not Jesus but we are his instruments are called to communicate Christ.

We are called to communicate Christ in all his glory.

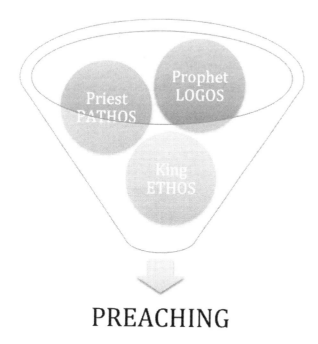

PREACHING

B. How Do You Grow in Style?

1. Pray and ask the Father to gift you and equip you.

2. Listen to others who are strong in the areas where you are weak and learn.

3. Use a coach to ask you good questions on how each style would deal with the passage.

↪ACTION ITEM: PREACHING STYLES

In Triads

Do you know "Who" you are?

Most of us are strong in one area with a secondary strength. Which one are you relying on the most?

- Are you, like a Prophet, someone who likes to tell the Truth?

- Are you Priestly, caring about the wounds, tender, focused only on adoption, not on any disciplines of grace?

- Are you a King who likes lists of things to do, principles to follow?

(Groups of 3—Church Planters discuss first)

Rate Your Style: (1=Not strong and 5= Very Strong)

1.   On a scale of 1-5, rate yourself as a Kingly preacher.

        1   2   3   4   5

2.   On a scale of 1-5, rate yourself as a Priestly preacher.

        1   2   3   4   5

3.   On a scale of 1-5, rate yourself as a Prophetic preacher.

        1   2   3   4   5

Discuss

1. When your mentors, professors, trainers, and your wife describe your preaching style, what have they emphasized?

2. When unchurched people comment on your preaching, how do they describe your style?

3. Name 1-2 practical (measurable, time related) steps you should take to improve your preaching style to communicate Christ in all His glory?

III. Your Model in Gospel/Grace Centered Preaching

Gospel centered preaching believes that Jesus Christ can change any person or institution through the power of his gospel. Gospel preachers let the gospel do its work. *"I am not ashamed of the gospel because it is the power of God for the salvation of everyone who believes"* (Romans 1:6).

A. Two Considerations:

1. What is Christo-centric/Gospel of Grace Saturated Preaching?

"No precise formula should instruct preachers how to maintain a Christ-centered perspective regarding the application of biblical truth. However, when people walk away from a message understanding that grace both motivates and enables them to serve God, futile human striving…vanish. Preachers, then, should make God's redemptive work the content, the motive, and the power behind all biblical exposition. Only when people look beyond themselves for spiritual health do they find their sole hope and source of power to do what God requires appear" (Bryan Chapell).

"To understand any particular text of the Bible, we must first put it into the 'micro' context—its historical and linguistic setting, in order to discern the immediate intent of the human author. But every Biblical text also has a 'macro' context—its place in the entire Bible, which has as its purpose the revelation of Christ as the climax of all God's redeeming activity in history. We must not only ask: 'what did the human author intend to say to historical audience"' but also 'why did God inscripturate this as a way of pointing to the salvation in his Son?" (Timothy Keller).

2. Whatever model you use will be related to how you answer the question, **"How Do People Change?"**

You already have an answer to this question. It is how you counsel, it is how you pastor, how you pray for people, and how you teach and preach. Jonathan Edwards said the purpose of every sermon was to take the Truth and make it real to people's hearts. In other words, the point is to facilitate the work of God the Spirit to transform the hearts and lives of those who listen.

In my years of listening to Gospel-centered preaching (I have had to listen to over 50 sermons each year), I have found there are least seven different models of those who are Gospel-centered.

You might adopt model and later change as you go. We are not advocating one over another. Each model is preaching Christ! Be careful you do not become critical of those who do not share your particular model and claim them not to be "Gospel-centered".

When you think of some of the better-known Gospel preachers today, you immediately realize that none of them are alike in their style or in their "gospel approach". Matt Chandler and Mark Driscoll are both A29 preachers—but they are very different. Tim Keller and Sinclair Ferguson are both Presbyterians, but very different. Mark Dever and Ed Stetzer are SBC, but preach differently. John Piper, Tim Keller, and Bryan Chapell are all Gospel preachers, but all very different in their model.

If you use the Gospel Coalition's resources site for preaching, you will find very different approaches to preaching the gospel. Now here's the point. Don't get confused by it all. There are different

"Gospel" preaching approaches. If you are new to preaching on a regular basis, it will take you awhile to find not only your style, but also your model. Remember, whatever model you follow it will answer how you believe God changes people.

Seven Models for Gospel-Centered Preaching:

1. Grammatical-historical Exposition

The grammatical-historical element deals with the nouns, verbs, tenses, cases, and all other pertinent exegetical aspects (i.e. syntax, use of idioms, metaphors, etc.). The *historical element* includes understanding the author's context, audience, and the overall purpose of the book as a whole.

"An expositor is solemnly bound to say what God says. In an expository message we relate precisely what a text of Scripture says. A more technical explanation—an old one that I hold to—is that an expository message gets its main points and its sub-points directly from the text. An expository message says what the text says and gets all its developmental features from the text as well" (Bryan Chapell, *Christ Centered Preaching*).

The goal with this type of preaching is to drain everything in the text out of the text. It means that you stay close to the text. GH Expository preaching is that which reminds the hearers of the relationship between the text you are preaching and the context of the book as a whole.

"Expository means that preaching aims to exposit, or explain and apply, the meaning of the Bible. The reason for this is that the Bible is God's word, inspired, infallible, and profitable—all 66 books of it. The preacher's job is to minimize his own opinions and deliver the truth of

God. Every sermon should explain *the Bible* and then apply it to people's lives. The preacher should do that in a way that enables you to see that the points he is making actually come from the Bible. If you can't see that they come from the Bible, your faith will end up resting on a man and not on God's word. The aim of this exposition is to help you eat and digest biblical truth that will: make your spiritual bones more like steel: double the capacity of your spiritual lungs: make the eyes of your heart dazzled with the brightness of the glory of God: and awaken the capacity of your soul for kinds of spiritual enjoyment you didn't even know existed" (John Piper).

What preachers come to mind that utilize this approach?

2. Repentance and Faith

This approach believes that repentance and faith are the two dynamics of spiritual change that God uses to produce transformation in lives. The solution to all problems is to repent of our self-sufficient/idol making life, and believe in Christ. The main emphasis is on the believers' adoption as sons and daughters in Christ.

Sermons can be expository or topical, but the solution always winds up being the lack of personal repentance and lack of believing in your position or adoption (sonship).

Martin Luther cautions: "So there are two parts of Christian teaching that we must emphasize for Christians daily. Neither faith nor works can be ignored. For when faith isn't preached—when no one explains how we are joined to Christ and become branches in him—then everyone resorts to their own works. On the other hand, if we teach only about faith, it leads to false Christians. These people praise faith, but they don't show any fruit or power. That's why it's so difficult to preach. No matter how I preach, something goes wrong. Someone always goes off on a tangent. If I don't preach about faith, the result will be useless and hypocritical works. If I only emphasize faith, no one does any good works. The result is either useless, faithless do-gooders or believers who don't do any good works…we must preach to those who want to remain in the Vine, put their trust in Christ, and put their faith into action in their everyday lives."

What preachers come to mind that utilize this approach?

3. Christ's Work is the Solution

"Christ-centered preaching rightly understood does not seek to discover where Christ is mentioned in every text but to disclose where every text stands in relation to Christ" (Zack Eswine).

This is sometimes referred to as the Redemptive-Historical hermeneutic. Christ is the power (reason) to obey and follow. His redemptive work is applied to a text, but it is not necessary to "find Christ" in every text.

"A passage retains its Christo-centric focus, and a sermon becomes Christ-Centered, not because the preacher finds a slick way of wedging a reference to Jesus' person and work into the message but because the sermon identifies a function this particular text legitimately serves in the great drama of the Son's crusade against the serpent" (Bryan Chapell, *Christ Centered Preaching*).

What preachers come to mind that utilize this approach?

4. Christ is Present in the Text

"We can define 'preaching Christ' as preaching sermons which authentically integrate the message of the text with the climax of God's revelation in the person, work, and teaching of Jesus Christ" (Sidney Greidanus).

"To understand any particular text of the Bible, we must first put it into the 'micro' context—it historical and linguistic setting, in order to discern the immediate intent of the author. But every Biblical text also has a 'macro' context—its place in the entire Bible which has as its purpose the revelation of Christ as the climax of all God's redeeming activity in history…There is, in the end, only two ways to read the Bible; is it basically about me or basically about Jesus?

In other words, is it basically about what I must do, or basically about what Jesus has done…? In the Old Testament we are continually told that our good works are not enough, that God has made a provision. This provision is pointed to at every place the Old Testament. We see it in the clothes God makes Adam and Eve in Genesis, to the promises made to Abraham and the patriarchs, to the Tabernacle and the whole sacrificial system, to the innumerable references to a Messiah, a suffering Servant, and so on. Therefore, to say that the Bible is about Christ is to say that the main theme of the Bible is the Gospel" (Tim Keller).

"Don't you know, young man, that from every town and every village and every hamlet in England, wherever it may be, there is a road to London? So from every text in Scripture there is a road towards the great metropolis, Christ. And my dear brother, your business is, when you get to a text, to say, now what is the road to Christ? I have never found a text that did not have a road to Christ in it, and if ever I do find one I will go over hedge and ditch but I would get at my Master, for the sermon cannot do any good unless there is a savor of Christ in it" (C. Spurgeon, *Christ Precious to Believers*).

What preachers come to mind that utilize this approach?

5. The Gospel Dance

"The Christian life is better seen, not as a two-step but as a three-step, a waltz! The life of the Christian is a continuous dance of 1,2,3; 1,2,3; 1,2,3. The three-step involves a lifestyle of repent, believe, and fight. The primary means of transformation is one of acknowledging our deep need for Christ through confession and repentance, and then looking to the power of the blood to be applied to our hearts by the Holy Spirit. But, once repentance and faith are exercised, out of faith, we do need to fight to be obedient" (Dr. Bob Flyhart).

"A deep change only happens when the Holy Spirit applies the grace of the gospel and brings 'despair' (repentance), over our doubt and disobedience then 'delight' (faith), over Christ's forgiveness and imputed righteousness and finally 'direction' – freeing us to follow his direction with a new affection, in worship, community and mission. The gospel of Jesus Christ tells me: 'I am perfectly accepted in Christ, therefore 'I obey' not 'I obey in order to be accepted'" (Dr. Tom Wood).

What preachers come to mind that utilize this approach?

6. Radical Free Grace

God the Father is no longer angry with you because of Christ and He will never be angry with you. His anger was poured out on his Son. He loves you. The greatest sorrow is to not believe He loves you. Principal realities are drawn from the Biblical text to affirm God's amazing grace. It's Jesus plus nothing that saves and motivates.

"Christians often speak about grace with a thousand qualifications. Our greatest concern, it seems, is that people will take advantage of grace and use it as a justification to live licentiously. Sadly, while attacks on morality typically come from outside the church, attacks on grace typically come from inside the church. The reason is because somewhere along the way we've come to believe that this whole enterprise is about behavioral modification and grace just doesn't possess the teeth to scare us into changing, so we end up hearing more about what grace isn't than we do about what grace is. The fact is that "Yes grace, but…" originated with the Devil in the Garden of Eden" (Tullian Tchividjian).

What preachers come to mind that utilize this approach?

G. Bad News/Good News

"The story of the gospel is the story of a Father whose children were seduced by the evil one. He is on an eternal quest to restore them to his family. So every sermon should include an explanation of the Bad News of how God's children were seduced and the Good News of the infinite degree to which God went to rescue his children…The entire message does not have to be evangelistic. There is a right place in every passage of

Scripture, and usually more than one place, to present the gospel. The Bad News; **sin**, **death**-spiritual, physical, eternal—and **works righteousness**. The Good News; **Love, Christ, Cross & Invitation**" (David Nicholas, *Whatever Happened To The Gospel?*).

What preachers come to mind that utilize this approach?

All of the above mentioned schools or models are antithetical to the moral based religious preaching that pervades the North American Protestant Church. Most of the moralistic models follow this line of thinking:

1. Here is what God says in the Bible that you must do.
2. Here are the steps of how you are to do what God has said in the Bible you are to do.
3. Now, go and work those steps and God will help you—and if you fail, he will forgive you.

Examine your own sermons and check yourself. What is the basic message you preach as to how people are transformed? Is it by the finished work of Jesus Christ, through his life, death, and resurrection or is it by our obedience and efforts to "live for Jesus" once we have believed?

"Why does Jesus matter? If you find that Jesus isn't pertinent to our content, you are probably teaching a great sermon on parenting, or giving, or moral uprightness or some needed act of service, but it isn't a gospel message. It's simply teaching people to try harder, to better follow this rule, and you can be your own savior…Jesus is what sets our points and our sermons apart. He isn't just the person we tag onto the end of our sermons, his work on the cross is the only way we can do anything…Pastors should move beyond Biblical principles to the gospel, bringing every message back to Gospel and Jesus" (Rodney Anderson).

> ⮡ ACTION ITEM: PREACHING SCHOOLS
>
> **Discuss in Triads**

1. Write out and discuss the following:

Circle the model of gospel preaching that is most familiar to you

Grammatical-Historical

Repentance-Faith

Christ's Work is the Solution

Christ is Present in the Text

The Gospel Dance

Radical Free Grace

Bad News/Good News

Discuss in triads

2. Describe the people in your context—race, socio-economic, education, political affiliation, religious culture, etc. How does that affect your preaching style and model you adopt?

IV. Your Audience in Preaching

A. Who you are <u>not</u> to be preaching to

Christianity, and especially conservative Christianity, is a sub-culture in American life. Most people today, though they may claim to be "Christian", do not share a biblical world-view.

So you are NOT preaching to the PCA, A29, EPC, SBC, AMIA, EFC, IPC or any other alphabet religious tribe. Those are all sub-cultures of the Christian-sub culture. As a Planter, you must force yourself to think of those outside any tribe. Gospel preaching is for both believer and non-believer.

If we fail to understand the culture we live in, we miss speaking to them within their "world view". We talk to ourselves, using our own nomenclatures, theological terms, arguing about issues that the average person (even churched person) does not understand, and much less care about.

Most people today do not know who Calvin, Luther, Packer, Spurgeon, Sproul, Stanley, or Keller are, much less understand why they are quoted as authorities in sermons. If you refer to Esther, Ezra, or Elijah, put them in context of the Biblical story and explain who they are. Assume you are speaking to intelligent people who are biblically and religiously illiterate.

B. Language is Vital

One of the most common mistakes today is to use undefined 'Christian-ese". Language is integral to our understanding of our world, new ideas, meaning, etc. Edward Sapir says, "Human beings…are very much at the mercy of the particular language which has become the medium of expression for their society." In short, language matters and it can be either a hindrance or a help to understanding anything in our society. The same holds true when one begins the process of entering newly into the community of faith.

Put yourself in the shoes of a non-Christian walking into your church. They hear words like *sin, faith, repentance,* or *redemption,* or phrases like "answer to prayer" or "sacrifice of praise". At best, they will have a vague notion of what they think these words mean. At worst, they will have no idea what you are talking about. In the secular conceptual language, there are no analogs for things like "sin" or "sacrifice of praise". We sound like aliens to them. "Sinful" is dark rich chocolate. "Decadent" sounds intriguing. "Wicked", if you are from Boston, means "awesome". Even "Gospel" to some people is a music style.

So, part and parcel to reaching our secular culture is helping them to understand the meaning of the "Christian language". We must define our terms and allow people the opportunity to see in the community of faith what "praise" looks like, or what "repentance" looks like.

German Philosopher, Ludwig Wittgenstein, uses the example of a chair: We understand what a chair is by virtue of our contact with chairs. They are things we sit in, we reupholster, we stand on to change a light bulb, we trip over in the dark, etc. Without these experiences, the term "chair" would be a vacuous concept.

Non-Christians will understand "answer to prayer" by participating in a community of faith in which prayers are boldly offered and answered, but also in which "prayer" is carefully defined in terms that are understandable to the outsider. The same goes for words like "sin" and "repentance". We must be careful to first define what those words mean, use them in ways that make sense to the non-Christian, and then be willing to live them out publicly.

To reach our post-whatever culture, we must understand that much of our vernacular is utterly foreign to the outsider, placing an unnecessary barrier to their coming into a life of faith in Christ.

Example: Think of the word "God". We know that we mean the Father of the Lord Jesus Christ, the sovereign Creator of all things, the lover of our soul, the Holy One, etc. He is the one we worship and submit to, on whom we depend, to whom we pray and confess. But what about the person who has never prayed, never confessed, never seen their life as anything more than living for the moment? To that person, the term "God" is, at best a single person deity or at worst, an empty concept! So we even have to define "God"!

If the "world" is the circle and your tradition is a dot in the circle, many of our preachers are preaching to the dot. I always counsel my Church Planter wanna-bes, **"Beware of the Dot."**

"At the very worst, evangelical preachers read and engage other evangelical preachers and writers. They read almost exclusively those thinkers that support their own views. Then sermons are really only helpful for…graduates of their particular stripe… At the best, evangelical preachers read and engage other evangelical Christians.

Then their sermons are really only helpful for other Christians. Christians may love the messages and feel they are being 'fed', but they know instinctively that they cannot bring non-Christian friends to church. They never think, 'I wish my non-Christian neighbor could be here to hear this'…If you spend most of your time in Christian meetings or in the evangelical sub-culture, your sermons will apply the Bible text to the needs of evangelicals…the only way out of this is to deliberately diversify your people context" (Dr. Tim Keller).

C. So who is in your audience?

Every time you preach, at some point in your message, you should prepare to speak to at least the following types of people:

• Skeptics, doubters, and cynics

• Seekers (all people are seeking something on which to orbit their life)

• Prodigals: religious prodigals (older brothers) or irreligious prodigals (younger brothers)

• Wounded

If you are new to preaching, you might want to list them in the margin of your notes as you prepare, and see if you can actually communicate your point to one of the people—just as if they were sitting across a table from you at a coffee shop.

"A man may be called to preach the gospel in the same place for years, and he may, at times, feel burdened by the thought of having to address the same audience, on the same theme, week after week, month after month, year after year. He may feel at times at a loss for something new, something fresh, some variety. It will greatly help such to remember that the one grand theme of the preacher is Christ. The power to handle that theme is the Holy Ghost; and the one to whom that theme is to be unfolded is the poor lost sinner. Now Christ is ever new; the power of the Spirit is ever fresh; the soul's condition and destiny ever intensely interesting. Furthermore, it is well for the preacher to bear in mind, on every fresh occasion to rising to preach, that those to whom he preaches are really ignorant of the gospel, and hence he should preach as though it were the very first time his audience had ever heard the message, and the first time he had ever delivered it. To preach the gospel is really to unfold the heart of God, the person and work of Christ; and all this by the present energy of the Holy Ghost, from the exhaustless treasury of Holy Scripture" (C H McIntosh, 1869).

V. Getting to Your Point

"If your spouse or roommate were to roll you out of bed at 3 A.M. and ask, "What is the sermon about this Sunday morning?" if you cannot answer in one crisp sentence, the sermon's not ready to preach. You need an idea people can grasp. If the sermon's idea is, "In the Babylonian incarceration of God's people, they suffered for seventy years to determine what God's plan was and never could determine it..." and you keep talking, that idea is not going to pass the 3 A.M. test. We need something like "God remains faithful to faithless people," something that's crisp" (Bryan Chapell).

Ask yourself:

- What is my message about? Every message should have a main topic or subject.

- Why is this message important? How will this make a difference tomorrow?

- What do any skeptics or unchurched people need to hear? What questions are they asking?

- What do I want them learn? Is there some action step? Belief, repent, and follow?

- What is my compelling point? Can you summarize it on Twitter?

- How is Jesus the Hero of the point? Is he the Hero in my action?

The Route to the Point: ala Andy Stanley (adapted from *Communicating for Change*):

- <u>ME</u> *Orientation*—finding personal common ground with the audience
- <u>WE</u> *Identification*—all of us here have dealt with this issue
- <u>GOD</u> *Illumination*—teach the Biblical text
- <u>YOU</u> Gospel *Application*—Jesus as motive and means to following
- <u>WE</u> *Inspiration*—What would happen if all of us embraced the big point?

The Point: ala Bryan Chapell (from *Christ Centered Preaching*):

- Identify the Fallen Condition Focus
- Specify the Christ Focus
- Discern the Redemptive Purpose
- Illustrate
- Apply

The Point: ala Tim Keller
(from Lecture Notes, "Preaching Christ in a Post-Modern World"):

AIM at heart-motivational level as well as behavior:

- The Plot winds up: **WHAT YOU MUST DO.**
  "This is what you have to do! Here is what the text/narrative tells us that we must do or what we must be." (Introduction; Our need for this teaching; build tension)

- The Plot thickens: **WHY YOU CAN'T DO IT.**

  "But you can't do it! Here are all the reasons that you will never become like this just by trying very hard." (A great place for story, honesty, brokenness, longings for glory)

- The Plot resolves: **HOW HE DID IT.**

  "But there's One who did. Perfectly. Wholly. Jesus the ____. He has done this for us, in our place." (Show the perfection/glory/beauty of Jesus so our hearts, not just mind/actions, are drawn after him)

- The Plot winds down: **HOW, THROUGH HIM, YOU CAN DO IT.**

  "Our failure to do it is due to our functional rejection of what he did. Remembering/receiving him frees our heart so we can begin to change.

No matter what route you take to the point, work hard on the Takeaway:

- Dig until you find it
- Build everything around it
- Make it stick

VI. Your Prayer in Preparation

If preaching is mainly or primarily communication, then we should place a high premium on techniques; but if we want to reach the heart (the motivational level), the reality is only God can reach the heart. One of the means God uses to penetrate the heart is *prayer*.

Martin Luther was asked if he had a choice between being a great preacher or a great prayer which would he choose. He said, a great prayer, because Jesus never taught his disciples how to preach.

"Your commitment to praying in your sermon preparation needs to be greater than your commitment to your mortgage payment!" (Steve Brown).

4 phases in prayer and preaching—keep them close:

- Private prayer in preparation
- Public prayer before you preach
- Public prayer after you preach
- Private prayer after you preach

➥ ACTION ITEM: PREACHING & PRAYER

In Triads

1. On a scale of 1-5, how much do you feel the need to pray privately in preparation for preaching? (1=Not strong and 5=Very Strong)

1   2   3   4   5

2. Discuss practical steps to renewing passion for private prayer.

3. In a typical sermon, rate yourself on a scale of 1-5 on how well you think you make a clear, memorable point? (1=Not strong and 5=Very Strong)

1   2   3   4   5

4. Discuss practical steps and helps for making sermon point(s) crisp and memorable.

VII. Practical Postscripts

A. Scheduling

1. You will have about 40-42 messages to do each year. Think about what you would like your church to know, what actions to take place, what ministries, what themes in life. What are your contextual applications? (52 weeks a year, minus vacation, guests, and special events)

2. Get out an annual calendar and lay out the holidays, vacations, guests, special services, mission's weekends, etc.

3. Lay out a MINIMUM of 4-6 week's worth of messages at a time. Again, think about themes in your context.

4. Consider using an annual theme for the first 3 years of your plant:

- Year One: Cause—Gospel and Mission—vision, mission, values of church, of Christianity, city
- Year Two: Community—Gospel Sanctification—growth in grace, Holy Spirit's gifts and fruits
- Year Three: Corporation—Gospel Cooperation—elders, deacons, ecclesiology

OR consider following the Liturgical Calendar. It will help assure that you cover the basic Gospel story every year.

B. Study rhythms

I. You have to learn how you prepare. When do you best think, write, and read? Is it in one stretch or divided up?

Here are some ideas—but follow your own learning rhythm not someone else's:

- Tuesday (4 hours)—Read text-passage; discover its meaning, outline, read commentators. Pray.
- Wednesday (4 hours)—Turn outlines & study notes into a sermon- move from what the text says into what the text says to us today. Ask God what He is wants to say.
- Thursday (2-3 hours)—Write it out in script.
- Friday (1 hour)—Preach it live to self- memorize the first 5 minutes of introduction.
- Saturday—Leave it alone.

OR

- Monday—Read the passage. Answer basic questions: what is it about, why is it important, what is the key idea? Ask God to show you what He is trying to communicate.
- Tuesday—Create a rough outline, with one of the 'getting to the point" ideas above.
- Wednesday—Write a script. Pray.
- Thursday—Re-write the script to make it better; no one gets it in the first draft.
- Friday—Preach it out loud. Pray.
- Saturday—Don't look at it.
- Sunday AM—Pray through it once more and then preach it.

2. When you have a schedule of thoughts, filing for messages will become easier. Keep 3x5 cards; as you listen to others, read, think, and as illustrations come to you, keep them filed.

3. Weekly preaching is one of the major challenges for Church Planters— most have never had to preach every week. Be wise with your time. Use pre-launch season for sermon prep.

C. Teaching Teams—Prep Together, Use Themes, and Share Stories

1. Using a team of people may help with prep time and in the gathering of sermon ideas and illustrations.

2. If you use a team in the first year, keep the lead church-planting pastor with the most preaching repetitions.

D. Place a Value on Being Coached

"Like Jesus, my coach understood that failure is a master teacher if it has a willing student" (Gordon MacDonald).

The following are some ideas for being coached in your preaching:

1. Pay someone, like a communications teacher, to listen to your messages.
2. Do NOT ask a homiletics professor from a seminary (no offense to anyone in particular).
3. People in the congregation are not good evaluators. Most of them are there because they already like it.

4. Your wife is not a good evaluator. She will either be too easy or too hard.

5. Consider asking your church planting coach to listen to your messages.

E. Practice

It takes 1,000's of hours to become truly great at anything. You will never get close to this unless you preach an hour-long sermon four times a week, every week, for life. But, you WILL IMPROVE if you practice. If you haven't preached regularly of course you need practice!

1. Set up a music stand in your office on Friday. Preach through your sermon until you can get all the way through it without getting "stuck".

2. You should expect to have to practice your sermon for the first 100 times you preach.

3. Memorize your introduction. You have 5 minutes to make them think your sermon has something they need before they 'tune out'. DO NOT WASTE THIS WITH CHIT CHAT.

"I felt that in preaching, the first thing that you had to do was do demonstrate to the people that what you were going to do was very relevant and urgently important" (M. Lloyd-Jones).

As people hear you preach, they ask: "Does this have anything to do with me? Is it pertinent to my situation, my family, and my work? Will there be something for me to take away from this?

You have to create tension. Work at asking great questions to provoke interest. They need to be thinking, "Yes I have had that question" or "Yes, please keep talking cause I have had that predicament too". "This is exactly what my friend needs to hear"; "This would help my non-believing friend's issue"; "My neighbor would get this."

F. Watch Game Film

Professional football players are required to look over game film every week. Athletes even watch every day's practice sessions…hours of their play to see how they will improve their performance.

1. Video record yourself and watch it. You should video record a minimum of 8-10 of your sermons.
2. Note annoying hand gestures, verbal expressions, pacing, etc.
3. Watch the video on fast-forward. This will highlight and reveal annoying habits that you might otherwise miss.
4. Note one thing about your delivery that you want to change and focus on correcting that one thing for the next time.

Remember, everyone can get better at this. Since this is your calling's craft, you should be diligent to do it well. However, also remember, preaching is NOT your life. Christ is your life!

Books and resources:

- Tim Keller, "Preaching Christ in a Post Modern World", Reformed Theological Seminary, iTunes

- Dennis Johnson, *Him We Proclaim: Preaching Christ from All of Scripture*

- Andy Stanley, *Communicating for Change*

- Bryan Chapell, *Christ Centered Preaching*

- Zack Eswine, *Preaching to a Post-Everything World*

- Paul Copan, *Is God a Moral Monster?*

- Ed Clowney, *The Unfolding Mystery*

- Jonathan Edwards, *A History of The Work of Redemption*

Shepherding God's People

Chapter Three

Caring for the community and the mission

Introduction

The goal of this module is for you to leave with a specific, dated plan for improving the shepherding of your church plant, however you call it in your context. There are two competing views within the 21st century evangelical church:

First View:

A pastor of a very large church in the USA said in an interview that the New Testament doesn't use the term shepherding after the gospels. The questions posed in the interview were:

Question: Should we stop talking about pastors as "shepherds"? Absolutely. That word needs to go away. Jesus talked about shepherds because there was one over there in a pasture he could point to. But to bring in that imagery today and say, 'Pastor, you're the shepherd of the flock,' no. I've never seen a flock. I've never spent five minutes with a shepherd. It was culturally relevant in the time of Jesus, but it's not culturally relevant any more.

Nothing works in our culture with that model except this sense of the gentle, pastoral care. Obviously that is a face of church ministry, but that's not leadership.

Question: Isn't **shepherd** *the biblical word for pastor?* It's the first-century word. If Jesus were here today, would he talk about shepherds? No. He would point to something that we all know, and we'd say, "Oh yeah, I know what that is." Jesus told Peter, the fisherman, to "feed my sheep," but he didn't say to the rest of them,

"Go ye therefore into all the world and be shepherds and feed my sheep."

By the time of the Book of Acts, the shepherd model is gone. It's about establishing elders and deacons and their qualifications. Shepherding doesn't seem to be the emphasis. Even when it was, it was cultural, an illustration of something.

What we have to do is identify the principle, which is that the leader is responsible for the care of the people he's been given. That I am to care for and equip the people in the organization to follow Jesus. But when we take the literal illustration and bring it into our culture, then people can make it anything they want because nobody knows much about it (Christianity Today, 2007).

Second View:

Pastor Tim Witmer suggests: "The fundamental responsibility of church leaders is to shepherd God's flock. After all, the word 'pastor' comes from the Latin word meaning 'shepherd'. However … shepherding is not merely the responsibility of those who are called to be pastors but also of those who are called to be elders or its equivalent in our churches" (*The Shepherd Leader*, 2007).

↪ ACTION ITEM

Discuss in pairs or Triads. Church Planters in the field answer first.

1. Which idea about Shepherding listed above most reflects your personal belief about Shepherding? Why?

2. List two or three key formal or non-formal ways you have been trained in the role of Pastor/Shepherd?

3. No matter how you define the role (shepherd, leader, elder, team) describe the system or strategies you have set up (or plan to set up) in your new church to care for the people God is placing under your leadership?

I. What is Shepherding? Is it still Biblical?

A. Definition

Shepherd, n.: 1. a person who herds, tends, and guards sheep.
2. a person who protects, guides, or watches over a person or group of
people. 3. a member of the clergy.

B. Biblical ideas

"Keep watch over yourselves and all the flock of which the Holy Spirit has made
you overseers. Be shepherds of the church of God, which he bought with his own
blood. [29] I know that after I leave, savage wolves will come in among you and will
not spare the flock. [30] Even from your own number men will arise and distort the
truth in order to draw away disciples after them. [31] So be on your guard!" (Acts
20:28).

"To the elders among you, I appeal as a fellow elder and a witness of Christ's
sufferings who also will share in the glory to be revealed: [2] Be shepherds of God's
flock that is under your care, watching over them — not because you must, but
because you are willing, as God wants you to be; not pursuing dishonest gain, but
eager to serve; [3] not lording it over those entrusted to you, but being examples to
the flock" (I Peter 5:1-3).

"Although the noun form of the word overseer (episkopos) is used only five times
in the NT (Acts 20:28; Phil. 1:1; 1 Tim. 3:2; Titus 1:7 and 1 Pet. 2:25) and the
verb form only three times (Acts 6:3; 1 Pet. 5:2 and Heb. 12:15), on three of those
occasions it is coupled with the noun **shepherd** *(poimçn, 1 Pet. 2:25) or the verb*
be shepherds *(poimaino, Acts 20:28 and 1 Pet. 5:2). This combination reveals*
that the overseer is informed and aware of the needs of God's people and responds

to those needs in the same caring fashion a shepherd would for his own sheep. Jesus is the one called "the Shepherd and Overseer (bishop) of your souls" 1 Pet. 2:25 (Tom Darnell).

C. Categories or Functions

Some think of Shepherding as Discipleship. Others talk about Shepherding in the form of a discipline team (termed a Shepherding Team), and still others refer to it in context of performing mercy care or emergency care.

So what is it in terms of function?

- Donald MacNair, in his book, *The Practices of a Healthy Church* (P&R Publishing), describes the shepherding principles as **Guardian, Overseer, Example, and Shepherd.**

- Timothy Laniak, in his book, *While Shepherds Watched Their Flocks: Rediscovering Biblical Leadership*, (Shepherd Leader Publications, 2007) uses the categories of **Provision, Protection, and Guidance.**

- Timothy Witmer, in his book, *The Shepherd Leader*, uses the categories of **Knowing, Feeding, Leading, and Protecting.**

These descriptions of Shepherding roles overlap. In various contexts, different Planters along with their spouse/family, may choose to modify the name, number and specific functions within a system. You may even use different terms, but the Bible is clear. Church leaders (elders) must perform the function of a shepherd and shepherds are leaders.

D. Practical Tips for Early Stages

It would be wise to set up some system that makes sense as a temporary means to shepherd in the initial gathering phase of a church plant. All responsibility for Shepherding is on the shoulders of the Planter until he puts something into place.

1. **Know your tendency**. Two early mistakes Planters face: Ignoring shepherding all together to focus on evangelism/mission or hyper-focusing on shepherding to the detriment of networking, evangelism and mission.

2. **Set a temporary system in place early**. Factoring in your natural tendency, your context (scratch or launch team, etc.), your progress and wise counsel from mentors and coaches, Planters need to set up some expectations and guidance for your start-up phase. Keep it simple. Explain it to your team and/or new people frequently.

Ask yourself: What is your temporary shepherding system? How are people cared for in our mission? Can your people explain it to others?

If you don't know it, you can be certain your people won't either. Don't fall into the Moses complex (Exodus 18) but be sure someone is sharing the responsibility and people know who is helping you and how.

II. Why and How Do You Shepherd Personally?

No matter your tendencies, your context or your system, all pastors are called to Shepherd in the following six ways in every stage of church planting.

1. **You are called to live your life as a model for others to follow.** You model what it means to be a father, husband, or grandfather—to model what it means to work for a living. You model a gospel life of godliness, faithfulness, and obedience to Christ. You model what it means to give generously. You have glorious opportunities to repent well and to "live a life of love."

2. Very few people (especially people in their 20's and 30's) have had worthy models of a man aggressively living out the implications of the Gospel. Very few know what it is to be really cared for and to be known, loved, confronted, forgiven, authentic, and accountable.

3. **You are called to protect from false teaching.** Paul warned the elders at Ephesus that wolves, thieves and false teachers would come in and ravage the people. People in the church are often clueless. Without a Shepherd-Leader, they will often fall away—"scatter" as Jesus put it.

4. **You have been commanded to care.** Jesus Christ, the Chief Shepherd, cared for his people. So must Church Planters. *"Be shepherds of God's flock that is under your care"* (1 Peter 5:2).

5. **You and your leaders must be personally involved in the lives of your people.** No one leads from a distance. Don't presume that if

you preach well, you are going to lead well. "Shepherding involves a personal relationship with specific people placed under our care by God himself. We must know them personally, extensively and intimately to ensure their spiritual health" (Thomas & Wood, *Gospel Coach*).

6. **You will need God to provide faithful, available and teachable people to assist you with Shepherding.** *"Jesus was moved with compassion because the crowds were harassed. He told his disciples, 'Ask (beg) the Lord of the Harvest to send out laborers into his harvest'"* (Matt. 9:35-38). As God brings people alongside you to work in the harvest, it is critical that you show them Jesus' heart for the crowds.

7. **You will modify and improve your Shepherding systems as you go.** Interaction and brainstorming will give the team agreed upon direction and expectations for Shepherding the crowd God sends you.

↪ ACTION ITEMS

Answer the following, then discuss:

1. On a scale of 1-5, how clear is (or was) your temporary Shepherding system in your own mind? (1=Not clear and 5=Very clear)

1   2   3   4   5

2. On a scale of 1-5, how clearly can your people explain Shepherding in your current stage of planting? (1=Not clear and 5=Very clear)

1   2   3   4   5

3. List the people who are currently helping you with Shepherding.

Discuss:

1. What is the #1 way you and your team need to improve Shepherding?

2. When will you next collaborate with others listed in #3 about improving or modifying the Shepherding plan in your church plant?

III. Four Shepherding Principles

What are you training people to do to help Shepherd others?

As you start the planting process and start gathering people, you will see the need to develop a temporary organization for shepherding that shares the work of shepherding. But what are you training people to do?

"A Gospel Shepherd brings all the issues, questions, needs, problems, or solutions to orbit around the sense of a Gospel dynamic, which he applies to each situation, because the Gospel is the ultimate solution for every problem" (Thomas & Wood, *Gospel Coach*, Zondervan 2012).

We suggest both informal and organized discussions and training centered on (1) Knowing, (2) Feeding, (3) Leading and (4) Protecting God's people through the Gospel.

A. Knowing God's People

Timothy Witmer rightly said, "It is our restored, loving relationship with the Lord that flows over into transforming our relationships with other people, particularly those who are also part of his flock.

We are exhorted in 1 Peter 5:2-3 to intimately know those who are under our care. The Holy Spirit has allotted to us or entrusted to us specific people that we are to know and shepherd. The English phrase translated in 1 Peter 5:3, "those in your charge" (ESV) or "those allotted to your charge" (NASB) or "those entrusted to you" (NKJV) is the Greek word kleros. According to scholars, kleros was an allotment of land assigned to a citizen by the civic authorities, the distribution frequently being made by lot" (*The Shepherd Leader*, 2007).

As we realize that the Holy Spirit has made us overseers of others' lives (Acts 20:28) and that God has entrusted us and assigned us with His sheep to know and to care for their souls, we will take our calling soberly and faithfully. When trouble arises, we must avoid the temptation to abandon our sheep or seek greener pastures for smarter/cooler/nicer sheep to shepherd.

Be sure to know the conditions of your flock (Prov. 27:23). This includes involvement—know the sheep. In order to know the "face" or the condition, the shepherd would look at the face of each sheep (after each day) to check for scrapes, cuts, ticks, eye infections, whatever might need salve or medicine.

Richard Baxter (ca. 1615-1691) suggested in his classic book, *The Reformed Pastor*, "We must labor to be acquainted, not only with the persons, but with the state of all people…what are the sins of which they are most in danger, and what duties are they most apt to neglect, and what temptations they are most liable to; for if we know not their temperament or disease, we are not likely to prove successful physicians."

Shepherding involves a personal relationship with specific people placed under our care by God Himself. We must know them personally, extensively, and intimately to ensure their spiritual health.

Dr. Tim Keller offered some insight on shepherd-leadership:

1. Shepherds inspect their flock (Acts 20:28).
2. Shepherds visibly care for their flock (Acts 20:31).
3. Shepherds diagnose their flock (Acts 20:20a).

We suggest a diagnostic of the following aspects of a person's life—RPMS:

- Relational diagnosis
- Personal diagnosis
- Missional diagnosis
- Spiritual diagnosis

Keys to Effective Shepherding in "Knowing":

- Spend time together.
- Be a good listener. James says there is ministry of healing by listening.
- Take their lives seriously.
- Try hard to understand with empathy.

"It is impossible to overstate the immense need that people have to be really listened to and to be understood by at least one other person" (Paul Tournier, *To Understand Each Other*).

B. Feeding God's People

You must feed God's people to provide spiritual nourishment and Truth. "Here I must take counsel of the Gospel. I must harken to the gospel which teaches me not what I ought to do (for that is the proper role of the law), but what Jesus Christ has done for me; to wit, that he suffered and died to deliver me from sin and death…the gospel wills me to receive this and to believe it. And this is the truth of the gospel. It is also the principle article of all Christian doctrine…most necessary it is, therefore, that we should know this article well, **teach it to others and beat it into their heads continually**"(Martin Luther, *Commentary on Galatians*).

We "feed the Gospel" to those who are following Christ by:

1. **Proclaiming**—*"For without faith it is impossible to please God"* (Heb. 11:6).

Nothing is more important for the Shepherd than to guide people back to God; to respond to God rightly in their times of need. Ninety percent of people have a low view of God. They struggle with the "Fight of Faith"; that is to believe God the Father, through God the Son, by the work of God the Spirit, loves them and is for them.

Concentrate on God's promises, not on their needs. Remind them of a resurrected Christ!

"The shepherd challenges and speaks into the life of the disciple, going after heart motivations. He probes issues regarding subtle idolatries such as church, work, success, or approval. He relentlessly proclaims the truth of the Gospel and its application into the life of the disciple, appropriately rebuking, reproving, and confronting the disciple to prompt him to align his living with God's truth. By declaring the truth, he feeds the disciple with meat and milk of the Word to develop a diet of healthy truth.

The shepherd relies on the Holy Spirit for the right words and tone at the right time; and is utterly dependent on Him to provide discernment to cut the disciple to the heart. But he does more than pierce the heart with truth. He also imparts great assurance in not simply the disciple's gifts, abilities, plans, and obedience, but in the Lord's promises. He sees current realities and issues, but also envisions and communicates the bright hope of God's call in the disciple's life…

He brings God and his glory and promises back into the big picture, continuously reminding the disciple-leader of the Gospel" (Thomas & Wood, *Gospel Coach*).

2. Praying—Pray for your people and pray with your people.

"Shepherds inspire the disciple with his own walk with God and dependence upon the Holy Spirit. The shepherd must look to the Holy Spirit as teacher, guide, sanctifier, and affirmer of our sonship and standing before God. He is our helper in prayer and the one who directs us and empowers our witness to a lost world" (Thomas & Wood, *Gospel Coach*).

Read Col. 1: 9-11:

"…We have not stopped praying for you. We continually ask God to fill you with the knowledge of his will through all the wisdom and understanding that the Spirit gives, so that you may live a life worthy of the Lord and please him in every way: bearing fruit in every good work, growing in the knowledge of God, being strengthened with all power according to his glorious might so that you may have great endurance and patience…" (NIV).

What you should be praying for the people?

1. That they would be **filled with the knowledge of His will.** Our prayer for them is that they would know and be filled with His Gracious design for their lives.

    Ultimately, the chief aim of all of life is for us to glorify God—tooffer back to Him the glory due His Name. We are to be enjoying life with God and others—to love God and love one another—in our relationships, in our personal lives, in our missional adventures, and in the inner spiritual life with God.

2. That they would have **all spiritual wisdom and understanding that God the Spirit gives.** The information they get from the Word has to have a life changing affect. It has to bring life transformation. According to Paul, there is a spiritual wisdom that becomes practical and life changing wisdom. There is a spiritual implication to their filling. In other words, the Gospel is taking root in them, through the work of the Holy Spirit!

Why should you be praying for your people in this way? In order that they:

- Live a life worthy or walk worthily. The idea of living life, in the marketplace, in the neighborhood, where they play or go out to eat. The spiritual wisdom helps them know the way they spend their time and their money. It gives wisdom as to the cars they drive, and the investments they should make.

- May please God in every way. They live a God centered life not a self-centered life. We are asking God to grow their new affections for God and find him better than everything else.

- Bear fruit in every good work. Here, he means that the fruit of spirit, love, joy, peace, patience, etc. is actually demonstrating itself in their new lives.

- Growing in the full knowledge of God. The greatest joy in life—the greatest treasure—is to know God. "God is the Gospel." What do we get through a gospel shaped life? We get God.

By what means is this accomplished in the lives of people you shepherd? **By being empowered by His power**—strengthened with power by His glorious might.

That is an amazing shepherd prayer for a means by which we feed the people under our care. We actually "pray it down" into their lives. We depend deeply on our Father who is able to accomplish more than we can imagine. Do we pray for people like this? Or do we settle for prayers about their safety and physical healing?

3. **Equipping**—Shepherds get people to practice doing.

    To "equip" (Gk. kartatizo), means to complete thoroughly; or to make mature. Our calling is to make mature followers (disciples) of Jesus Christ for the work of service, building up the Body (Ephesians 4:11ff).

    Members of the Body are to do the work of ministry and you are to equip them!

Four biblical definitions to describe getting people practicing what they hear:

1. Mending their nets (Mk 1:16, 19; 4:21).
    The fishermen had to make sure their "nets" were kept up. The idea is that we are continually preparing ourselves for use. To change metaphors, it is like keeping the saw blade sharpened for use. Basically, we equip by training, coaching, and developing new leaders.

2. Bring to completion (I Cor. 1:10).

    Here, Paul uses the idea of bringing a conflict to completion. To be joined together after a fractured relationship. Any relational conflicts are resolved. We are called to be peace makers not peace keepers. We are reconcilers.

3. Complete what is lacking (Thess. 3:10).

    Here the idea of equipping involves adjusting the shortcoming of their faith and their understanding of the Gospel; faith, repentance, obedience.

4. Restore (Gal. 6:1).

    Here Paul suggests that equipping means him coming alongside them; he equips them by encouragement; idea is strong of restoration from hardship.

Key Diagnostic Questions for a Healthy, Growing Church Plant:

- Are you or your staff doing all or most of the ministry?

- Are the people doing the ministry?

- If you want more people involved, the primary question isn't, "What can we do to get people more involved?" The first questions to ask are: Are we equipping people to do ministry? Are we making disciples? Are we giving them opportunity to do ministry?

> **⮩ ACTION ITEM**
>
> **Answer the following in writing (3 minutes), then discuss in 2s or 3s (Church Planters go first)**

1. List the means (activities, events) your team currently utilizes to get **to know people?**

2. List plans or current practices you and/or your team have to **feed the people by prayer?**

3. List plans or current practices, *other than sermons*, you have to **feed the people by proclamation?**

4. List plans or current practices you and your team have to **feed the people by equipping?**

Discuss

1. Which of the above plans or current activities need the most attention now?

2. When will you discuss this with your team?

3. What kinds of specific help or coaching do you need to help you with your shepherding plan?

4. Where will you get the help you need?

III. Four Shepherding Principles (continued)

C. Leading God's People

"Leading the flock is a key responsibility of the shepherd. 'He leads me beside still waters. He restores my soul. He leads me in the paths of righteousness for his name's sake'" (Psalm 23:2–3).

"Shepherds usually **lead by walking in front of the flock** with an occasional look behind them, utilizing a whistle or special call to keep the flock in line" (Thomas & Wood, *Gospel Coach*).

To be a skillful Shepherd you will, at times, have to adapt your preferred leadership style to ensure that His flock is healthy and secure. Resist the temptation to say "Well, that's just the way I am" to excuse your unwillingness to adapt your leadership to the situation.

A Shepherd may need to lead with tender, pastoral care, providing rest for the weariness of his flock. Other times, there might be the need for bold direction, while other times it will be **leading by influence**. Shepherds **push from behind** to avoid distractions and trouble and sometimes may be guides by just "being there" with the disciple.

1. The nature of being a leader in the church is spiritual.

<u>Overseer</u>: In Acts 20:17, Paul "summoned" the presbuteros (or elders) to listen to him. He said, "The Holy Spirit has made you 'episkipos' or bishops" (v. 28). Bishop and elder are used interchangeably in the New Testament. This requires that you "watch after", in a good way, the people in your charge.

I Tim. 3:1, Paul suggests that being leader has a very high degree of personal responsibility to the community of faith. It is a noble (kalou) task, meaning it is worthy or honorable work.

This is not so much the idea of title but of function. In our culture, we tend to think title, but this is not title or age. To rule, manage, oversee the church and its functional life. This role entails leadership in everyday practice: it is function.

Tim Witmer relates a story about a group of tourists in Israel whom their Israeli tour guide had informed, after observing a flock and their shepherd, that shepherds always lead their flocks from the front. He told his attentive listeners that they never "drive" the sheep from behind. A short time later they drove past a flock along the road where the shepherd was walking behind them. The tourists quickly called this to their guide's attention and he stopped the bus to discuss with the "shepherd." As he boarded the bus he had a sly grin on his face and announced to his eager listeners, "That wasn't the shepherd, that was the butcher" (Tim Witmer, *The Shepherd Leader*).

Your position does not give you authority. Function may get you respect and spiritual authority, but your authority, though ordained by God, is still given to you by the people as you steward that leadership.

2. The nature of being a leader in the church is practical and accountable to God.

<u>Steward-leadership</u>: "Christian steward-leaders function in a "household", that is, in an extended family. Therefore we say that a steward-leader does the work in community, a community of which he or she is a part. The church is God's "household" (Gal.2:10) and family

(Eph.2:19; 3:15). We are not ultimately a business, (though the financial donations of God's people are a resource that requires faithful and responsible stewardship as well.) So the job of the steward is not only to seek the goals of the master and strategically deploy resources. He or she must also build and maintain a real community where all this is accomplished. Relationships of truth and love must be maintained while we are cultivating the Lord's resources for him" (Tim Keller, unpublished paper, "Biblical Theology of Church Leadership").

You were made an "Overseer" by the Holy Spirit, to care for the flock (metaphor for God's people), to oversee (carefully watch) them, which <u>He purchased by His own blood</u>. It is NOT your church; it is His.

D. Protecting God's People

Protecting means to provide defense against sinful behavior and errant doctrine (wolves disguised as sheep). Your call is as a Shepherd; to protect or guard the flock of God.

"Shepherds function in a protective role. They acknowledge that the disciple is wrestling daily with doubt, fear, pride, and idolatry. They understand the natural propensity of the disciple-leader is to relate to others, to his work, to his marriage, in ways that might serve his desire for approval, comfort, and security. The shepherd as protector diagnoses possible subtle ways that sin is invading the disciple's heart and affecting his approach to life. He will remind the disciple of God's love, Spirit empowerment, and sovereign reign in his or her life.

"Sheep are completely defenseless in their natural environment. They are not the fierce defenders of their domains. They are furry and cute and have limited senses. Their only defense is to flock together with other sheep. A lone sheep will surely be killed without the protective (and constant) oversight of the shepherd" (Thomas & Wood, *Gospel Coach*).

We protect by personal and interpersonal involvement. This involves both your personal shepherding and getting people involved with other Christians to do life together: care, love, pray, teach, encourage—all the "one anotherings" of Scripture (Matt. 18:15,16).

The key passage for shepherds to protect the people: *"We ask you…to respect those who are over you in the Lord and who admonish you…"* (I Thess. 5:12-14).

The Apostle Paul writes, ***"We ask you"***. "Ask" is a strong word, meaning to urge, request, entreat, beg, beseech:

1. **"Admonish the disorderly",** verse 14 (ESV). The Greek word for "admonish" is "noutheteo", meaning to confront strongly the disorderly, meaning those who are undisciplined, insubordinate, or busybodies. The word "disorderly" (ataktos), is like a soldier who is "not keeping in the ranks."; it is about those who are out of line.

In context of love and relationship, you **MUST move toward them**.

Read this Rule of St. Benedict, Benedictine Monastery, 6th Century: "If any pilgrim monk come from distant parts with wish as a guest to dwell in our monastery and will be content with the customs which he finds in this place, and do not perchance by his lavishness disturb the monastery, but is simply content with what he finds; he shall be received for as long a time as he wishes. If indeed he find fault with anything or expose it reasonably and with humility and charity, the Abbot shall discuss it prudently, lest perchance God has sent him for this very purpose. But if he has been found gossipy or divisive in the time of his sojourn as the guest, not only ought he not be joined in the body of the monastery, but also it shall be said to him honestly that he must depart. If he does not go, let two stout monks, in the name of God, explain the matter to him."

Admonishment summarized:

- Love them hard and well, but be bold and proactive.
- Problems do not go away by themselves.
- When it comes to church discipline, follow Matthew 18 and pay careful attention to your denominational steps for formal discipline.

2. Encourage the fainthearted. Come alongside the timid, frightened, and negative thinkers. Instead of blasting those who have been neutralized in their life, befriend them and "put courage back" into their lives.

3. Help the weak. Hold up people who have given up, who are wounded or hurt, or have quit or have been overcome by some addiction, until they are able to stand on their own again.

4. Be patient with everyone. That will drive you to the Gospel and to one another, because there are plenty of folks in the church who have Borderline Personality Disorders. The church will be filled with men and women who have ruined their lives and make continue to make nasty decisions.

➥ ACTION ITEM:

Answer in writing (2 minutes), then discuss in pairs or triads (Church Planters go first)

1. List the means (activities, events) your team currently utilizes **to lead the people?**

2. List plans or current practices you and/or your team have to **protect the people?**

Discuss

1. Which of the above plans or current activities need the most attention now?

2. Do you need specific help or coaching? Where will you get the help you need?

3. When will you discuss this with your team?

IV. Shepherding Models—Build a Community!

We are on the home stretch. Now that you have been wrestling with the why and how to Shepherd, we will give you some approaches and templates to take back to the field to start improving the Shepherding in your church plant.

A. Resist the Therapeutic Approach.

Henri Nouwen offered this critique: "Few ministers and priests think theologically. Most of them have been educated in a climate in which the behavioral science, such as psychology and sociology, so dominated the educational milieu that no true theology was being learned. Most Christian leaders today raise psychological and sociological questions even though they frame them in scriptural terms.

"Real theological thinking, which is thinking with the mind of Christ, is hard to find in the practice of ministry. Without solid theological reflection, future leaders will be little more than pseudo-psychologists.... They will think of themselves as enablers, facilitators, role models, father or mother figures, big brothers or big sisters, and so on, and thus join the countless men and women trying to help their fellow human beings cope with the stresses and strains of everyday living. But that has little to do with Christian leadership" (*In The Name of Jesus*).

B. Build on Christian Community.

"It is our conviction that the gospel word and the gospel community do not fail us when it comes to pastoral care. Together they provide a secure framework within which to approach pastoral issues.

"We often think of pastoral care simply as something that takes place in moments of crisis. But most pastoral care takes place in the context of ordinary life—as we eat together, wash up together, play in the park, walk along the road. This preventative care often averts pastoral crises or helps people cope when they face difficult circumstances. But for these to be occasions of pastoral care we need to be intentional about encouraging and exhorting one another with the gospel" (Tim Chester & Steve Timmis, *Total Church*).

C. Define and Know Your Parish.

Thomas Chalmers, pastor of St. John's, the poorest parish in Glasgow, was given free rein to try his schemes to make the parish the hub of spiritual care, education, and help for the poor.

He wanted everyone to have a church (1) near enough, (2) at seat rents low enough, and (3) with a district small enough to be thoroughly cared for. He divided the parish of 10,000 into manageable areas and appointed deacons and elders to visit families.

D. Spread the Load—Deploy the Right Shepherds .

I encourage you to read *Gospel Coach*, a book that I co-authored with Scott Thomas. In the book, we list "5 Characteristics of a Good Shepherd":

1. **Compassion (love).** "Jesus had compassion because they were harassed and helpless like sheep without a Shepherd" (Matthew 9:36). Love for Jesus and love for His sheep are essential to effectively shepherd another person. Without this characteristic, the relationship will be clinical, professional and will lack Gospel transformation.

2. Courage (faith). The Shepherd pursues the disciple in his or her rebellion, apathy, or sin and holds them accountable for purity of life and doctrine. We must have the courage to confront others in love as a regular pattern of our relationship. We must be willing to enact discipline toward their actions when necessary (Matthew 18:15-17). They need us and want us to regularly monitor the fences in their life.

3. Contact (community). A Shepherd is an "Overseer", watching for deviancy and a disciple's tendency to escape or wander away in isolation. Jesus told the parable of a man with 100 sheep and one of them that went astray. He suggested that a good Shepherd would leave the 99 others and search for the one that wandered from the fold (Matthew 18: 12–13). The Shepherd knew the lone sheep was gone because he had regular contact with the wandering one.

4. Calling (passion). Every believer is called to make disciples. Shepherds must examine their hearts, their motivation, and the cost to their lives, as they follow this calling. When you have confirmed that calling, you must passionately pursue God's glory by obeying your calling.

5. Commitment (generosity). Shepherding others requires a generous commitment of time, relational energy, and focus. We can't shepherd others halfheartedly. God rebuked this lack of commitment, "The weak you have not strengthened, the sick you have not healed, the injured you have not bound up, the strayed you have not brought back, the lost you have not sought, and with force and harshness you have ruled them. So they were scattered, because there was no shepherd" (Ezekiel 34:4-5a).

↪ ACTION ITEM:

Answer the following in writing (5 minutes)

1. Take 3-4 minutes and review the decisions and notes you made during this training. Jot down here 2-3 applications.

- In the next 6 days I need to:

- In the next 6 weeks I need to:

- In the next 6 months I need to:

2. Who will hold you accountable and ask you how these changes are being implemented?

3. Does that person know they are holding you accountable? If not, when will you discuss this with them?

VI. Operating Strategies—Potential Ideas for Providing Pastoral Care

The following outlines provide potential templates for team discussion, decision, and accountability for the flock entrusted to your care.

The model or Shepherding strategy you choose will most likely be determined by your context (place, size of congregation, etc.) and your personal preference or leadership style. We are not advocating one strategy over another. You must understand that the people God has placed under your leadership need to be cared for by leaders/shepherds. It is a stewardship issue.

Size matters. For a church size of 40 to 199, consider the following:

"While relational dynamics are now less intense, there is still a strong expectation that every member have a face-to-face relationship with every other member. While there are appointed leaders and elected leaders, the informal leadership system remains extremely strong. There are several lay people—regardless of their official status—who are 'opinion leaders.' If they don't approve of new measures the rest of the members will not support them.

The pastor is still primarily a shepherd. While in a larger church, the people will let you pastor them if you are a good preacher, in a smaller church they will listen to your sermons if you are a good pastor. Effective, loving shepherding of every member is the 'driving force' of ministry— not leadership or even speaking ability. A pastor who says, 'I shouldn't' have to shepherd every member, I've delegated that to my elders or small group leaders is trying to practice large church dynamics in a small church environment" (Tim Keller, *Cutting Edge Magazine*, Spring 2008).

A. The Shepherd Leader Model (Tim Witmer)

Seven Essential Elements of an Effective Shepherding Ministry

1. Must be Biblical—what biblical foundations dictate who should Shepherd?

2. Must be systematic—you must have a strategy to care for the people.

3. Must be comprehensive.

4. Must be relational. Delegate to the flock:
   - by geographical area
   - by fellowship groups—mini-congregations (you can have two elders over each "congregation" or one elder and one deacon)
   - by small groups—small group leaders (men & women) are trained to care
   - by elder "draft" selection—elders select the people they want to shepherd by natural lines of relationships already established; include deacons (Acts 6)

5. Must include the four Shepherding functions—Knowing, Feeding, Leading, and Protecting.

6. Must include accountability monthly accountability—each elder gives update on his oversight annual diagnosis.

7. Must include prayer.

B. The Shepherd Group Model (Ralph Neighbor, *The Shepherd's Guidebook*)

A. Shepherding groups—Cell Church Model
   1. Your flock should never be more than 15 people
   2. Your ministry to them is to guide them to discover their gifting/calling
   3. Your ministry is to provide care
   4. Your ministry is to pray for each one

B. Each cell has a shepherd leader and an apprentice

C. Accountability for group to an oversight leader over all cells

C. Discipleship Model

"The officers must come to the realization that their key Biblical role is that of shepherd of the flock (1 Pet 5:2) and be willing to be freed up from board work in order to focus more on that role. And to truly shepherd as Jesus did, they must learn what it means to truly disciple others in a "life-on-life" fashion (for more on this, see www.transform-coach.com on "Transforming Discipleship").

"Those that do serve on the board must give up the right to micromanage the Pastor and be in on all the key ministry decisions. However, they must become committed to the role of providing more true governance oversight of the results of the ministry" (John Purcell, *Turning Your Church Board into a Great Strategic Asset: Are You Ready for a Radical Change in Church Governance*).

D. Small Group Model

Friendship Ratio: 1:7

Each new person should be able to identify at least 7 new friends at church within the first 6 months of their attendance.

Group Ratio: 7:100

At least seven relational groups should be available for every 100 in attendance.

New Group Ratio: 1:5

Of every five relational groups, one should have been started in last year.

If less than 50% of your first time visitors do not return for a second visit, analyze your whole worship service experience. If 25% or less remain, analyze your infrastructures. For instance, do you have enough small groups or personal connections for people to stick and feel cared for by someone and/or some group?

In larger churches, small groups provide people a community where they care for one-another, pray for each other, celebrate life, serve, and build close knit friendships. The leader is seen as their lay-pastor or Shepherd. Each small group leader is trained to be the "Shepherd" of his/her group. They provide care, prayer, friendship, and encourage ongoing spiritual community. The pastor encourages the congregation that the church is designed to provide pastoral care not through the professional clergy, but through the trained leaders in community groups. Small group leaders are provided regular ongoing support, coaching, and training in order to provide quality shepherding of those placed in their care. Small group Shepherds provide home and hospital visitation, prayer times, counseling, service/mission opportunities, encouragement, and may even conduct funerals for those in their "flock".

Each small group is a flock of no more than 12 people (married and singles), and not less than 4. Every church member is expected to participate in a small group in order to receive the feeding, leading, and protecting they need.

E. Parish Model

"It's no surprise that in this fragmented world, community becomes a higher value, even though it is so darned hard to achieve and sustain. Throwing a small-groups program at this hunger for community is like feeding an elephant Cheerios, one by one. What's needed is a profound reorganization of our way of life, not a squeeze-another-hour-for-"community" into the week. Perhaps many of our churches will become more like Catholic churches in the past, where the ideal parish had a few households where monks or nuns lived in community, practicing radical hospitality that would overflow to the community at large. Perhaps we'll find that if even a few people in our churches practice this radical hospitality and generous community, their extraordinary fervency will warm us all and model new ways of life for us manic, transient, auto-driven denizens of bedroom non-communities" (Emergent Church Leader, Brian MaClaren, *Christianity Today*).

In the Parish model, the church draws geographical lines of their respective community (parish). All people living in that geographical community are members of their parish, regardless of whether they are members of their church. The leaders and members work to get to know each household in the parish and provide prayer and assistance. They seek to learn the needs, concerns, and names of the families. They form partnerships with other services and community focused ministries and services.

"The heart of each neighborhood congregation is a network of **missional communities**: mid-sized groups (25-40 people) that meet throughout the neighborhood and provide the ideal environment for building relationships while connecting to the heart and mission of the church. To join a missional community is to enter into the journey of Christian discipleship. The missional community is essential, as it keeps the church small enough for everyone to have a real identity and be involved in the work of ministry, each using her own gifts to build the church. Missional communities are organized around a shared mission to a neighborhood or industry. They cultivate partnerships with schools, organizations that provide social services, business leaders, activists, community organizers, and anyone else who loves his city and wants to make it a better place to live; they then leverage those partnerships to implement strategic projects aimed at redeeming and renewing that neighborhood" ("The City Parish", Trinity Grace Church, NYC. www.trinitygracechurch.com).

What are the marks of a Parish congregation?

1. *A regional identity*—The Parish congregation has a vision and plan for ministering to a region that is a self-identified unit (e.g. downtown as opposed to the entire region). This region, interestingly enough, seems to be always roughly encompassed by a six-mile radius from the parish Church.

2. *A collegial staff*—The Parish congregation is staffed by clergy who have primary pastoral care for distinct congregations/parishes within the overall minister structure. The congregations are resourced by the

clergy but have local leadership in place. This provides a balance for clergy: between direct pastoral care, and the development of specialty ministry areas (based upon giftedness) that minister to the entire Parish (e.g. teaching, counseling, etc.).

3. *A training center*—The minister's missional focus and larger span of care is to raise up people who are called to ministry who can receive very hands-on practice tied to theological reflection. The Parish church's mission keeps in check the tendency for pastoral interns to become overly focused on intellectual pursuits to the detriment of actual ministry to people.

4. *Flexible facilities*—Central offices of the Parish church could provide meeting space, specialized equipment (e.g. recording studio, video production, etc.), bookstore, library, health center, mentoring programs, classroom space, and even room for commercial or non-profit development.

5. *Missional stance*—The driving purpose of the Parish church is innovative ministry to a non-Christian culture. It provides a way to share integrated word and deed ministry to a specific region by distinct (yet connected) local congregations/parishes (Sam Wheatley, *New Parish Models*).

F. Solo-Pastor of Smaller Church Model

"I created a prayer guide with each member of the church broken into a 28 day chart in alphabetical order. This is to represent the first 28 days of each month. On day 1, I pray for those 5-6 people or families. Then, I try to make some kind of personal contact with them that day in the form of a home visit, email, hand written card, phone call, Facebook note, or text message to let them know I prayed for them on that day. Lastly, I ask in that moment of personal contact if there is anything I can do to serve them. For those I haven't seen recently, I will usually call or go see them to get an update on how they are doing in general.

I repeat the same process for day 2, then day 3…all the way to day 28. If I am faithful and consistent in this process (which I never do perfectly) I would have prayed and made contact with all those who have been entrusted in my care in one month. Any extra days of the month I do the same thing with our missionaries and others we have sent into ministry from our church.

This became such a fruitful system to keep up with all our folks that I took it to our elders and they began to do it also. It became such a fruitful system for each of us as elders that we made a chart for our members and encouraged them to pray for each other in the same way as a prayer guide for our church. Several of the members have even adopted the model to contact folks that day they pray for them. It has been amazing the fruit that has come from many of our members taken this task to pray for one another seriously.

On our women's retreat last month, one of our dear ladies in the church led our ladies in a project to take that chart and transfer it to index cards that can sit on their table at home in the form of a flip calendar. Each morning, you just flip to the next day and you see who you are to be praying for that day. Since putting this on the table in our home, our children now make an assertive effort to pray for those appointed for that day" (Brian Croft, Senior Pastor, Auburndale Baptist Church , Louisville, KY and is the Founder and Ministry Development Director of Practical Shepherding, Inc. This is from an article in *Gospel Coalition*).

G. Congregational Care Model

The purpose of the Shepherding Program at First Church is to improve the level of pastoral care of the congregation by the utilization of lay members as caring shepherds. The desired result of the program is that each member of the congregation feels that they are vital part of the church.

The Shepherding Program will provide a new communication link between congregational members and the officers at First Church. The Shepherding Program will also provide a vehicle for smaller groupings of the congregation's members (e.g. Youth, Women of the Church, Men of the Church) to offer and supply support to one another as they learn of sickness, bereavement and other crises.

DUTIES OF SHEPHERDS

1. Become acquainted with each member of your group.
2. Contact members of your group regularly by phone and at church.
3. Relay information to the minister so they are informed and can be responsive.
4. Relay certain needs to the Youth, WOC, MOC, Minister, Elders, Deacons, etc. so they can be responsive.
5. Listen actively.
6. Be a one-person welcoming committee to greet members of your group at worship and other church events.
7. Pray for the members of your group regularly.
8. Pray for the success of this Shepherding plan.

SHEPHERDING ACTIVITIES

1.   A letter will be sent from the pastor to the congregation and "friends of the church" explaining the Shepherding Program.

2.   Each Shepherd is to contact the members of his/her group by personal visit, letter or phone establishing the first contact about the Shepherding Program.

3.   Speak with each member of your group at least once a month. Establish rapport so that each of you will feel at ease and be able to talk freely about any concerns that they may have.

4.   Find out when their anniversaries are, birth dates, etc. Send them a card!

5.   If you don't see them in church for a few Sundays, call them to see if they are ill, disturbed about something, etc.

6.   Have their birthdays, anniversaries, etc. published in the Digest.

7.   Greet them each Sunday at church. Sit with them at worship.

8.   If a member of your group does not drive, volunteer to provide transportation for them.

9.   If there is a young couple with children in your group, baby sit one evening so that they may have a relaxing dinner date.

10. If a member of your group doesn't drive anymore, take them for a drive.

11. Send a card to any in your group who may be ill or bereaved.

12. Be in prayer for those who are ill or bereaved.

13. If a member of your group is not very active in church activities, encourage them to become so.

14. If a member of your group lives alone, visit them, take them to dinner, and have them to dinner at your house. Pick them up if they don't drive.

15. Pray for the success of this Shepherding Program.

16. As you obtain information about bereavement, death, etc, pass it along to the appropriate committee.

17. Pass along to the Youth Coordinator any needs of the elderly or infirmed for yard work, visits, errands, etc.

18. Keep the pastor informed of any needs you may find.

19. Men of the Church have had work days in the past to help rake leaves or do small repairs. If you find any needs of a member of your group, pass it on to the Men of the Church.

20. If a member of your group is a "care giver", give them a break. Sit with the one for whom they give care so they can take a "time out."

> ↪ **SUMMARY ACTION POINT**

1. Using the previous page as a template (or another you prefer), formulate an improved shepherding idea for your church or mission that you will present as a potential to improving your church's Shepherding.

2. With your coach or supervisor, set a date by which you will:

- Finish the one-page suggested plan for improvement _____

- Inform the co-leaders in the plan _____

- Announce the plan to your group or congregation _____

- Review with team _____

3. Put those dates on your calendar and to-do list.

Time Management for Church Planters

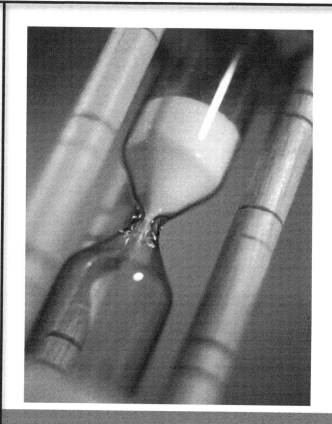

Chapter Four

Time is life

Introduction

Many Church Planters do not have a personality type that is highly structured. They have to live by the motto—Semper Gumbie—"Always Flexible". And they like it that way. One of the many struggles in planting a church is the lack of structure. If you have come from an established church, with staff and staff meetings, elders meetings, team meeting, and reporting, the transition to solo Planter with no weekly commitments (you have to create your own schedule each week) might be a real challenge.

Managing your time and life is a stewardship issue. It is important for us to not only make the most of every opportunity in our life, but also invite the people we are leading, evangelizing, discipling, teaching, and encouraging to become better stewards of their lives as well.

In this module, we want to explore, evaluate, and re-engineer our lives and (in particular) how we use our time to make the most of our life. We all get the same amount of hours or the same number of turns around the globe. You will only have this one season in your life to launch this particular church. Your kids will only be this age right now. There will be no "do-overs" in this season.

---

1. On a scale of 1-5, how would you rate your personal ability to manage your schedule? (1=What is a schedule? and 5=Excellent)

1   2   3   4   5

2. On a scale of 1-5, how would you rate your desire to be more effective in time management? (1=Poor and 5=Excellent)

1   2   3   4   5

3. What are your biggest time wasters?

4. What are you currently doing to manage your time?

5. What could you be doing better to manage your time?

6. If you got one thing from this module that would help the most, what would that be?

Introduction Continued

Ephesians 5:16 Paul commands his listeners, to *"Make the most of every opportunity"* (NIV**)**. Translated in the old KJV, *"Redeeming the time wisely"* and in the ESV, *"Making the best use of the time."*

What is interesting is that Paul does not use the word <u>Kronos</u> for time, meaning chronological or sequential time. Kronos time is measured by clocks (hours, minutes, and seconds). It is the time in which we make appointments and face deadlines. We schedule our lives by it.

Instead, Paul uses the word, <u>Kairos,</u> meaning the idea of the season of your life. "Kairos is the right moment of opportunity which requires proactivity to achieve success. It is significant and decisive. These moments transcend kronos, stirring emotions and realities to cause decisive action. It is not an understatement to say that kairos moments alter destiny. To miscalculate kronos is inconvenient. To miscalculate kairos is lamentable…Tolkien provides some clarity about kairos decisions throughout his epic. The hobbits, the elves, Gandalf, the Fellowship are all part of a meta-narrative; a story that provides framework upon which other's experiences can be built.

Each of us is afforded moments to take a stand, regardless of appearance (Frodo, the Hobbit) to position (Aragon, the king in waiting). Kairos moments can catapult a person into the very essence of life, which often comes with great consequences. Yet, it is there, in kairos moments, where we live the great drama of life. Maybe it is in those times when we feel most alive, most in touch with our eternal purpose" (Mark Freier).

Two approaches to time:

1. **Time-oriented or structured people.** Time conscious people are busy, hardworking people, racing from one event to another: meetings, appointments, phone calls, emails. Life is scheduled. They live and die by their Outlook calendar, iPhone, or Blackberry.

2. **Event-oriented people**. These people are busy as well, but they tend to not be time conscious—in fact some might not even wear a watch. These are people who more or less go with the ebb and flow of life.

Some of you adapt and change depending on the setting. Most likely you have a preference. Both complain about busyness of life—hustle and bustle. Both say things like, "Oh man there isn't enough time in a day." And the common solution is "Take a time management class or get a planner to get handle on your schedule."

But the problem is NOT time management.

The problem is not that you need to move from old school paper and pen day planner to a digital planner. It may not be that you need better skills for time-management (some might need it). It's real easy to be busy (appointments, bills to pay, kids schedules, counseling, sermon preparation, etc.) and not be wasting a moment of time because you have scheduled every hour correctly, but end up wasting your LIFE.

Stewardship of time seems to be one of the more difficult areas of the Church Planter's life. Time must be a servant to the calling of your life. Traditional time management theory suggests that by doing things more efficiently, you'll eventually gain control of your life and that increased control will bring personal fulfillment. But increased efficiency does not necessarily help facilitate the objectives that lead to the fulfilling of your calling.

If you are a time-conscious person, you might be solid in your clock management. But is great clock management a means to an end or an end in and of itself? If you are more event-oriented, you might say you don't care really, but you often feel scattered and ill-prepared. And that causes anxiety.

Instead, it may be helpful to answer the following questions that are referenced in my book, *Gospel Coach*:

1. What are your stated goals?

2. What do you actually do with your time?

3. What is most important in your life to do?

4. What can you eliminate from your life that is taking time away from doing the most important things?

Here is bottom line. Everyone is living for something.

Whether you acknowledge it or not, you are living for something. There is **something** that is your ultimate value; something that gives you meaning and a sense of joy or wholeness for life. It might even be a good thing.

Getting your life more scheduled to attain your personal goals won't deal with what is driving your life/heart. You are doing what you want to do. For many Church Planters, it's that the church succeed.

Point: **People do what they love to do** (paraphrase of Jonathan Edwards).

You are structuring your life, managing your time/life, to do what you ultimately love because we spend our time on things we ultimately love. If you feel overworked at your plant, it might be that you are living for something that is driving you instead of God leading you. Let's dig in.

I. The importance of Personal Values in Using Your Time

"Resolved, never to lose one moment of time, but to improve it in the most profitable way I possibly can"(Jonathan Edwards, *Resolutions*).

●————————————————————————————●

Most Church Planters overestimate what they can accomplish in the first year of their project

●————————————————————————————●

A. Everybody lives for something.

It's not what we *say we value*, but what we are *ultimately doing with our lives* (time, relationships, money, etc.) that reveal what we are really living for and what we really value.

B. Values matter most.

Our personal values are our *convictions regarding what we believe are important and desirable*. Values are important because an understanding of one's personal values is useful for time management. Most of us have the opportunity—not to mention the encouragement—to do more things than we'll ever have time to do. Consequently, we need to wisely select the tasks that we'll work on. A clear picture of our personal values allows us to rank the tasks on our "to do" lists according to how closely each task is associated with what's really important to us.

So, our values will influence our time priorities, choices, and actions more than we realize. There are things we consider most valuable to us and we show lots of emotion about them. Our attitude toward them is a window into what we value. What we think about, pray about and dream about can also reveal what is most important and valuable to us. What we admire about others is another window to reveal what we value.

Pray your personal values into your life and practices. Make them part of your prayer calendar, maybe taking one value for each day of the week.

➥ ACTION ITEM: ASSESSING VALUES

Self Exercise, then discuss in leadership groups

1. What are three personal values you deeply want to live out in your context? Discuss them with your leadership group.

    1.

    2.

    3.

2. How often do you read over your values? Do you pray them down into your life?

II. Time and Your Life Mission

**"If you don't change what you're doing,
you'll keep getting what you're getting".** (Unknown)

A. Your life mission statement should be memorable and liveable.

Here is a sample: "My life mission is to enjoy life in the freedom of the gospel of Jesus Christ by finding Him as my greatest life; by being a loving, caring, and concerned husband, father, and friend. To be there in those relationships that I have through supportive, instructional and serving ways and by kindly offering the gospel to those who are without hope."

B. Church Planters are called on a mission that is cross-cultural to some degree.

Church Planters need to discern and adapt accordingly to the differences in views of time (lateness, efficiency, usefulness of time, participation and flexibility) but also keep redeeming the time God has given for His mission in that context.

Groups, settings, traditions and generations can have a variety of opinions and values about time that conflict with each other. Your home church may be very time-oriented while the people you seek to reach are far less time-oriented. These differences require understanding and flexibility in both personal leadership and group leadership.

Church Planters balance both self-leadership that 'redeems the time' and group leadership that adapts to distinctions within your context.

C. Church Planters lead and influence multiple groups and subcultures in a variety of settings.

How will you make the most of your time and reach your context? How will you adapt your personal preferences among a variety of groups with differing views of time?

In their book *Ministering Cross-Culturally: An Incarnational Model for Personal Relationships* (Baker, 1986), Lingenfelter and Mayers state that most individuals and groups are somewhere between the two poles of 'Time-orientation' versus 'Event-Orientation' **and state that both are valid** (emphasis mine).

One cannot expect others to adapt first. So Church Planters should learn to notice *unstated differences and expectations* while interacting with various groups:

- o You are "late" if you are not 5 minutes early to speak at city council meetings.
- o You are not "late" to poker night if you get there within 20 minutes of the stated time.
- o You are not "late" to a party at a co-worker's if you are within the hour.
- o You are "late" to a party at your Anglo boss' house if you are not more than 15 minutes late.

- Continually adapt personal expectations, even with groups of similar cultures and backgrounds.

- Recognize that a distinct church culture forms with the people who join your mission during the early phases of the church plant.

Discerning and assigning value to the importance of lateness, efficiency, and relationship can lead to clearer communication, avoid misunderstanding and address potential conflicts before they arise.

D. Like Jesus, Church Planters must incarnate into the time attitude of the people we are sent to reach while making the most of the time God gives us.

Christ, the eternal Son of God, entered the constraints of time and space, followed His Father's plan to the letter, did all that was required of Him, and accomplished exactly what was needed.

While we will never perfectly replicate Christ's model, by the power of the Gospel, through dependent prayer and the power of the Holy Spirit, we are called into a selfless, life-giving ministry for the sake of others.

↪ ACTION ITEM: ANALYZING INDIVIDUALS

Self Exercise

1. On the continuum below, mark the time/event orientation preferences of the key individuals, groups and sub-cultures with which you work now or will work in the future. Remember to mark yourself, spouse, supervisor, coach, landlord, neighbors, co-workers, launch team, leadership group, cultural influencers, city or neighborhood organizations, home church, schools, cross-cultural groups in your context and anyone or any other group that is mission critical.

Time Orientation   Event Orientation

2. Analyze the time/event orientation of your context. Are your time/event preferences affecting outreach and making friends with more people outside the church? If so, how? In what ways will you need to adapt?

3. Analyze the time/event orientation of your support structures (home church, financial supporters, leadership group, network, supervisor, coach). What, if any, adaptations do you need to make?

4. Anticipating making disciples and developing leaders, what (if any) adaptations in your schedule will need to be made for the mission to grow healthy? How will time expectations for potential leaders need to change?

> **ACTION ITEM: ANALYZING "SUCCESS"**
> **Answer the following and then discuss**

1. On a scale of 1-5, how would you rate your personal wrestling with proving yourself through your plant and how much time you give to it? (1=Poor and 5=Excellent)

1   2   3   4   5

2. On a scale of 1-5, how would you rate your desire to be known for the size of your church?
(1=Low Desire and 5=High Desire)

1   2   3   4   5

Discuss:

1. Since the success goddess or size idol usually drive a lot of our time, what is the #1 way you can keep idols of the heart from overcoming you?

2. When will you next collaborate with your coach about this gospel issue?

III. The Most Important Roles You Have

"The key is not to prioritize your schedule but schedule your priorities."

Your life roles are not a list of priorities. Life is not "Jesus, Others and You". A Gospel-centered approach to life is not following a list. We are called to love God and love our neighbor. They are not in sequence. We love God by loving our neighbor (spouses, children, friends, etc). Your role as a church-planting pastor (elder/shepherd) interfaces with all other roles and, in some respect, informs the others (i.e. I shouldn't be an elder if I am not loving my wife as Christ loved his church). Also, there should be a sense of convergence in these roles and not living life in a silo or compartmentalized fashion (i.e. "Time with my kids is from 7-8 PM, Monday, Wednesday and Thursday"). Don't separate family from church life.

However, in terms of managing your life's schedule, it is helpful to lay out the most important roles you have to be sure you are loving God in the ways he has commanded and not in the ways you choose. Life includes a holistic life: Relational, Personal, Missional, and Spiritual aspects (RPMS).

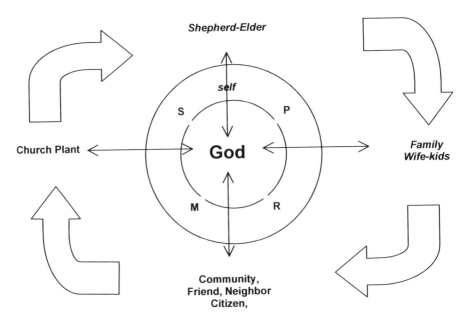

> ↪ ACTION ITEM: ANALYZING RESPONSIBILITIES
>
> **Discuss in pairs or triads (Church Planters go first)**

1. Given the church planting context and season you are in, what are 5 of your top responsibilities you have now? If you do not do these 5 things, the mission will not be accomplished.

2. What are two or three ways you would like to see the work of the Holy Spirit more clearly in your time management?

3. What place in your life do you give to prayer?

IV. The Four Quadrants

A. The Four Quadrants in Life Management

Priority Setting Illustration:

In his book *The Seven Habits of Highly Effective People*, Stephen Covey identifies "putting first things first" as vital for getting the most important and excellent things accomplished. There is a need for a paradigm shift in how we set priorities.

The following is an illustration from his seminar using big rocks, pebbles, and water to be extremely clear (or you can search YouTube for a variety of versions):

Our life and time is like a large clear container with a limited capacity that can be filled up with a variety of sizes of rocks, pebbles and water, each representing quadrants: Q1-Q4 priorities.

Next to the bucket-shaped container are other symbols:

- 8-10 BIG rocks labeled with Q1/Q2 priorities (urgent client meetings, major planning for future, community involvement, family time, vacation, rest, church commitments, etc.)
- A sizable container full of tiny pebbles representing Q3 priorities (urgent but not important)
- A pitcher of water representing Q4 time-killers

To start, all of pebbles (Q3) and water (Q4) are poured into the larger container representing one's life. This fills up to about 2/3rds capacity.

An audience member is then asked to get the remaining BIG rocks into the bucket without going over capacity. Easy to imagine, it is a messy attempt and in the end impossible, right? Some important but not urgent priorities simply will not fit.

But what if the same quantity of rocks, pebbles and water are placed in the container in a different order?

First, place all the BIG rocks (Q1 and Q2) in a fresh container, then the pebbles (Q3) fit around the BIG rocks, and then some of the water (Q4) can fit as well. In the end, setting priorities enables it all to fit.

What do we learn? (Hint: there is not always room for more)

Start with the big rocks first, based on our values, our life mission, and roles.

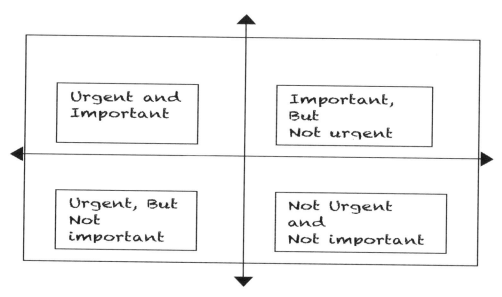

Four quadrants diagram

1. Quadrant I: Urgent & Important

These activities include crises, pressing problems, and deadline driven issues. These are things that need your immediate attention and you have to deal with right now. Quick fix. Intervention is key word.

2. Quadrant II: Not Urgent & Important

These activities include relationship building, long term planning, strategic planning, professional development and personal development. These activities nurture your whole person, help you develop your present ministry or develop a plan for future ministries. Prevention is key word.

Time management experts believe you should try to spend more than 50% of your time in Q2 activities in an effort to grow, learn, renew, and form meaningful relationships.

3. Quadrant III: Not Important & Urgent

These activities include interruptions, some calls, some email, some reports, and meetings. This Quadrant is full of interruptions or calls that others consider pressing and urgent but may not be as important to you.

4. Quadrant IV: Not Important & Not Urgent

These activities include trivial non-productive busy work, some email, junk mail, and some unsolicited cell calls. These are time wasters, such as unplanned television watching or Internet surfing.

➥ACTION ITEM: MAKING CONTACTS

Self Exercise, then Discuss in Pairs or Triads (Planters go first)

Write each task in the appropriate matrix quadrant from pages 116 & 117.

TASK LIST:

Prepare a sermon

Work on training materials for leaders

Complete year-end report for mother church (two days overdue)

Complete Launch Team manual (due in three days)

Have lunch with Bob

Talk to Jim about possibility of taking on worship service project

Answer email

Read article sent by A29 via Twitter direct message with post 'Will change your ministry 4ever!'

1. Evaluate the current activities you are doing in Quad 4.

2. List all the current activities you are doing in Quad 3.

Discuss

1. What important work in Quad 2 must fit into your schedule?

2. Evaluate how you set priorities. How can you begin to rearrange, plan, and organize your life to put first things first?

3. What good things are you doing that prevent you from doing the most excellent things?

V. Planning Your Life Wisely (Ephesians 5:16 Not as unwise, but wise)

A common issue facing many Planters is that the boundaries between work and ministry (church plant) are very blurred. If you office out of your home it is accentuated. **If you do not plan the use of your time someone else will.**

A. Time Management in the Changing Phases of Church Planting

1. **Phase One: "Conception".** Church Planter Assessment to moving to the field. Issues for which you have to manage time include:

    - Completing your church planting proposal
    - Completing your funding: writing potential support partners, making calls, visiting donors
    - Recruiting 100 prayer supporters, answer email responses
    - Relocation issues: securing housing needs, moving
    - Family issues: helping kids find schools, doctors, meeting neighbors
    - Personal Life: exercise, fun, rest, mental development
    - Spiritual life: reading Scripture, prayer, community, family spiritual renewal

2. **Phase Two: "Pre-natal".** Core/Launch Team development to first public worship. Issues for which you have to manage time include:

    - Completing your strategic plan
    - Prayer meetings and prayer walking
    - Personal evangelism (30-40% of time should be used in evangelistic networking)

- Networking in community
- Cultivate relationships with "not yet" or "unchurched" Christians
- Building your Launch Team
- Leadership team development
- Finding a worship facility
- People gathering events
- Making Disciples
- Sermon planning and worship scheduling
- Dating wife and recreation with kids
- Personal Life: exercise, fun, rest, mental development
- Spiritual life: reading Scripture, prayer, community, family spiritual renewal

3. **Phase Three: "Birth"**. Post Launch of public worship.

Issues for which you have to manage time include:

- Networking in community
- People gathering
- Personal evangelism
- Developing key ministry leaders
- Disciple making
- Sermon preparation
- Worship planning
- Staff meetings
- Counseling
- Dating wife and recreation with kids
- Personal life: exercise, fun, rest, mental development
- Spiritual life: reading Scripture, prayer, community, family spiritual renewal

B. Common Time Wasters

"Business expert Peter Drucker said that he has yet to see an executive, regardless of his or her position, who could not get rid of 25% of the demands on his time without anybody noticing. In other words, most of us should be able to eliminate 25% of what we do with our time and it will not have a detrimental impact on our work" (Thomas and Wood, *Gospel Coach*).

In *Gospel Coach*, Scott Thomas and I describe the following list of things that will rob your time:

1. **Personal interruptions:** How can we effectively steward our time to avoid these? First of all, be firm. When someone asks you if you have "a minute," ask about their agenda and see if there other people that could possibly talk to them. Block out time to focus for long periods of time on the most important things in your life. If you work with others in an office setting, agree on a "quiet hour" where you do not interrupt each other.

2. **Phone calls and text messages:** Learn to set a personal callback time for phone messages, and use voice mail options when you have them available. With cell phones, this is an even bigger problem. In the past, receptionists were able to filter incoming calls and take messages. Now, with text messaging, Skype, and the innumerable people who have your cell phone number, it is tempting to answer every incoming call and text. You may feel guilty if you ignore a call.

3. **E-mail barrages:** Organize your e-mail to screen for junk messages. Unsubscribe from unwanted e-mail lists. Schedule two to three times a day to check and respond to e-mails and stick to your rule. On-going e-mail work distracts you and keeps you from being productive.

Learn to use the two-minute rule. If you can handle the e-mail within two minutes, do it. If not, file it and schedule a later time to deal with it. All of your incoming or sent messages that you absolutely need to keep are kept in one file. Don't be an email hoarder. You can digitally search more efficiently in this way. Keep your inbox empty at the end of each day.

4. **Message alerts and phone ringers**: Let me suggest turning off the message alert on your e-mail to keep you from losing your focus. When working on important projects, turn off your phone ringer or close your door with a sign saying, "I'm working on an important deadline, I'll be free at 3:15pm."

5. **Short attention spans**: We must learn to focus. Some find it helpful to use instrumental music or white noise to help quiet their mind while working. Use headphones to block out noise when working in a busy place, and lastly, set up your workspace so that your back is to the traffic flow if you are easily distracted.

6. **Social media:** Twitter and Facebook have added a new doorway into our lives that can cause constant interruptions. Social media is an important portal to communicate and to lead, but it comes with added pressure to respond to other's posts and updates. Learn to be proactive in your social media engagement rather than reactive to every comment made on your social media account. Use it as a tool and not as an open door to interrupt. I set aside a total of five minutes a day on Facebook and two minutes on Twitter.

7. **Your daily energy cycles:** Be aware of how your workflow affects your energy level and decide on the best time of the day to tackle an important project.

C. Time (Kronos) Savers

We don't really "save time" because time keeps on ticking on into the future.

- Keep a capture list: as the day goes on capture all the calls you must make or tasks that must get done

- Delegate more than you do

- Say "No" to more than you do

- Pray more than you do

- Whenever you are asked to add something, think: what will I stop doing?

One Church Planter confessed that there were 3 hours that would radically improve his life:

- If he would wake up one hour earlier
- If he would come home to his family one hour earlier
- If he would go to bed one hour earlier

He had to ask the Spirit to give him the willingness and the ability to change his life to fit his values. The reason being, the church plant had subtly taken over his life. His calendar was a Gospel issue.

↓ACTION ITEM: OWNERSHIP

Self Exercise, then discuss in Pairs or Triads
(Church Planters go first)

Using your own calendar or the one attached, lay out the big blocks of your weekly schedule based on your values, your life mission, your roles and responsibilities in your particular church planting phase. Calendar your necessary sacred times. Plan for margin!

By logging your time, you can spot the habits that zap your effectiveness, including the major time wasters.

		Sunday	Monday	Tuesday	Wednesday	Thursday	Friday	Saturday
7	:00 am / :30 am							
8	:00 am / :30 am							
9	:00 am / :30 am							
10	:00 am / :30 am							
11	:00 pm / :30 pm							
12	:00 pm / :30 pm							
1	:00 pm / :30 pm							
2	:00 pm / :30 pm							
3	:00 pm / :30 pm							
4	:00 pm / :30 pm							
5	:00 pm / :30 pm							
6	:00 pm / :30 pm							
7								

> ↪ ACTION ITEM: SUMMARY
> **Self Exercise (5 minutes)**

1. Take 3-4 minutes and review the decisions and notes you made during this training. Jot down 2-3 applications.

- In the next 6 days I need to:

- In the next 6 weeks I need to:

- In the next 6 months I need to:

2. Who will hold you accountable and ask you how these changes are being implemented?

Does that person know they are holding you accountable? If not, when will you discuss this with them?

3. With your coach or supervisor, set a date by which you will:

- Review your current schedule _____

- Submit a revised time management schedule _____

- Review the new schedule with coach _____

4. Put those dates on your calendar and to-do list.

5. Pray for one another in your group.

Missional Engagement: Part 1

Chapter Five

"**Missional Engagement**: Church leaders recognize that the only acceptable offense is the offense of the gospel in all their interactions. Missional engagement for them is both effectively sharing the gospel and leading others in outreach. They are skilled in applying the resources of the church to the social needs of others. They affirm God's common grace in all people. This conviction enables them to effectively gather people, embrace diversity, and engage in mercy ministry" (Dr. J. Allen Thompson, *The Church Leader Inventory, Dimension 3*).

INTRODUCTION:

For most of us, being an Evangelist is work. Some of it is due to our own perception of what an evangelist looks like or how he behaves. Yet, as veteran Church Planter Shayne Wheeler said, "Your church as a whole will not love non-Christians or be committed to reaching them with the Gospel any more than you are. You are the pacesetter for personal and corporate evangelism in your church. Period. No excuses."

> ↪ ACTION ITEM:
>
> **Self Exercise (5 minutes)**

When you think of a doctor, what image comes to mind? When you think of an American cowboy, what does he look like? How about a NFL middle linebacker? If you described a computer techie, or rock star, what would come to mind?

Now, write out a description of an Evangelist. What images come to mind?

Introduction continued

Did you put down slick talker in white shoes, waving a big black Bible, yelling and sweating? Maybe you thought of a picture of Billy Graham, in a stadium, making an invitation while the buses wait. I suspect that many have a dim view of an Evangelist.

The hurdle for us to be Evangelists might begin with our own bias. We hold wrong views of evangelism. Nothing may be more daunting in your church plant than evangelism. But as you enter a new city as a Church Planter, you must see yourself as a Missionary-Evangelist.

When Jesus told his disciples to go into the world and be witnesses, he hit the "Send" button. John Stott wrote, "This sense of having been sent was a fundamental awareness of Jesus. It had a significance, urgency, and compulsion to everything he did…If God was to Jesus, 'he who sent me', then Jesus must be to us, 'he who sent us…" (*The Lord Christ is a Missionary Christ*).

We have been commanded to go and be witnesses of a risen Christ who is able to save to the uttermost. It is work though, and it means that we have to be intentional in our relationships, conversations, lifestyles, and in creating an exceptional community of believers that is "being the church".

The early followers of Jesus knew this "gospelling" and understood it as the most effective means of communicating the reality and good news of what had happened: The King, God himself, had come in the person of Jesus of Nazareth to inaugurate a new kingdom and way of life! God was committed to restore all things to himself through Jesus, the Christ! He had commissioned his followers to be witnesses to and messengers of, this good news, through words and deeds that were consistent with that reality and teaching.

We may struggle with being Evangelists because of the inertia of fear. Let's face it: there is a cultural taboo about being too radical with one's faith. There can be an atmosphere of scorn, ridicule, or outright opposition. There remains a conspiracy of hostility for Christ. Spiritual warfare is real.

We may also struggle with a sense of pride. We do not want to be looked down on by business leaders or neighbors. We may look foolish or overly religious. We would rather be acceptable in our religious endeavors.

In this module we will consider what the gospel is and what a Missionary-Evangelist looks like as he enters the mission field. I do not want to detract from the high calling and valuable station of the pastor/teacher/shepherd—so please do not misunderstand—but the call to plant a church is a missionary calling to be an Evangelist. Some denominations specifically identify the Church Planter as an "Evangelist", not "Church Planter" or "Organizing Pastor".

We can say that the primary function of a Church Planter is to evangelize lost people and Christians with the Gospel—that "Christ died for sins according to the Scriptures, that he was buried, that he was raised on the third day according to the Scriptures" and those who turn away from self saving forms of trying to right their enslaved and sinful lives and believe the historically true Gospel, will be reconciled to God. Evangelists have confidence in the Gospel.

The call to Church Planting is a call to go to a mission field of people that do not know God. It is not a call to go and care for the ninety-nine sheep already in the fold! What is your calling?

In Missional Engagement: Part 2, we will consider how the leader creates an evangelistic culture in the new church that will invade and saturate the lives of your community and missionally practice Christianity in word and deed. For now, let's consider your own personal calling as a Missionary-Evangelist so that your city or region will begin to see a "Gospel spring"!

I. What is the "Evangel" or Good News?

A. Biblical Considerations

"Now, brothers and sisters, I want to remind you of the gospel I preached to you, which you received and on which you have taken your stand. [2] By this gospel you are saved, if you hold firmly to the word I preached to you. Otherwise, you have believed in vain. [3] For what I received I passed on to you as of first importance: that Christ died for our sins according to the Scriptures, [4] that he was buried, that he was raised on the third day according to the Scriptures" (1 Corinthians 15:1-4).

"As for you, you were dead in your transgressions and sins, [2] in which you used to live when you followed the ways of this world and of the ruler of the kingdom of the air, the spirit who is now at work in those who are disobedient. [3] All of us also lived among them at one time, gratifying the cravings of our flesh and following its desires and thoughts. Like the rest, we were by nature deserving of wrath. [4] But because of his great love for us, God, who is rich in mercy, [5] made us alive with Christ even when we were dead in transgressions — it is by grace you have been saved" (Ephesians 2:1-5).

"But now apart from the law the righteousness of God has been made known, to which the Law and the Prophets testify. [22] This righteousness is given through faith in Jesus Christ to all who believe. There is no difference between Jew and Gentile, [23] for all have sinned and fall short of the glory of God, [24] and all are justified freely by his grace through the redemption that came by Christ Jesus. [25] God presented Christ as a sacrifice of atonement, through the shedding of his blood — to be received by faith. He did this to demonstrate his righteousness, because in his forbearance he had left the sins committed beforehand unpunished — [26] he did it to demonstrate his righteousness at the

present time, so as to be just and the one who justifies those who have faith in Jesus" (Romans 3:21-26).

"For Christ also suffered once for sins, the righteous for the unrighteous, to bring you to God. He was put to death in the body but made alive in the Spirit" (1 Peter 3:18).

B. Theological Considerations

In *The Westminster Confession of Faith and the Catechisms* there are definitions on sin, justification, adoption, sanctification and glorification, but there is no one definition for the Gospel.

The Gospel is more a story than it is a definition. In other words, to explain it you have to tell a True Story.

"The Story of the gospel is the story of a Father whose children were seduced by the evil one and now the Father is on an eternal quest to restore them back to his family" (David Nicholas, *The Gospel Bootcamp*).

All of us should have a working outline of the Gospel that we can adjust to the needs of the hearer.

↪ ACTION ITEM: YOUR GOSPEL SUMMARY

Self Exercise (3 minutes)

Write down your "elevator" version (a short version you have to tell on an elevator ride) of the Gospel. How would you explain it to someone who asked you, "What is the Gospel?"

Some speak of the Gospel in terms of *God, sin, Christ,* and *faith*. Others use the story-arc of the Bible and speak of the gospel in terms of *creation, fall, redemption,* and *restoration*.

Dr. Steve Childers, President of Global Church Advancement, writes of the Gospel story:

> First, the king had to come. Approximately thirty years before Jesus made this announcement, 'the kingdom of God is at hand', he, as the eternal Son of God, broke into human history and took on humanity (John 1:1-14). That is good news, but the good news is about more than his birth. The Scriptures also tell us the good news of his life. From infancy Jesus entered into personal battle with every spiritual enemy that had defeated his people and held them captive. As a warrior-king, he lived the life we should have lived. He faced every temptation known to man from the world, the flesh, and the devil.
>
> The good news is that, unlike you and me, he never sinned. In so doing he earned a perfect righteousness before God, completely obeying all of God's commands in thought, word, and deed. However, the good news is more than about his birth and life. The good news is that as our king, Jesus offered himself up as more than our life substitute. He also became our substitute in death. When he died on the cross, he did not simply experience the pain of physical suffering and death. He also suffered the full wrath and punishment of God that we deserve because of our sin.
>
> The good news is that he not only lived the life we should have lived, he also died the death we deserved to die. However, the good news is about even more than his birth, life, and death. The

good news is also that God raised him from the dead and has now seated him on the throne of heaven and thereby given him the sole authority and power to deliver his people from sin's captivity. Because of Jesus' birth, life, death, and resurrection almost two thousand years ago, God has now made him Savior and Lord.

Therefore Jesus' lordship must be seen as a direct result of His death and resurrection. When the apostle Peter first preached the good news, he said that Jesus had been "raised from the dead and . . . exalted to the right hand of God" (Acts 2:32-33). This symbolic statement that Jesus is now at the right hand of God is meant to teach us that Jesus is presently reigning and ruling in heaven as both Savior and Lord. As Savior, he alone has the authority and power to deliver people from sin's penalty and power over their lives. As Lord, he alone has the authority to demand that everyone, everywhere, submit to his rule over their lives (Acts 17:30).

The apostle Paul said, "Now he [God] commands all people everywhere to repent. For he has set a day when he will judge the world with justice by the man he has appointed" (Acts 17:31). The good news is that this exalted Christ is coming again (Matt 24:30; 25:19, 31; 26:64; John 14:3), and he is going to bring all things under his rule" ("True Spirituality," unpublished paper).

"What was this good news that Paul preached? It was the news about Jesus of Nazareth. It was news of the incarnation, the atonement and the kingdom—the cradle, the cross and the crown—of the Son of God. It was news of how God 'glorified his servant Jesus' (Acts 3:13) by making him Christ, the world's long awaited 'Leader and Savior'. Acts 5:31" (J. I. Packer, *Evangelism and the Sovereignty of God*).

C. Various Confusing Gospel Summaries

"'The good news is God wants to show you his incredible favor. He wants to fill your life with 'New Wine' but are you willing to get rid of your old wineskins? Will you start thinking bigger? Will you enlarge your vision and get rid of those old negative mind-sets that hold you back?

'The good news is that God's face will always be turned toward you, regardless of what you have done, where you have been, or how many mistakes you've made. He loves you and is turned in your direction, looking for you'" (A critique quoted from *Gospel Bootcamp Manual*, David and Eleanor Nicholas, 2012).

D. Various Church Leaders' Gospel Summaries

Tim Keller: "The gospel is: you are more sinful and flawed than you ever dared believe yet you can be more accepted and loved than you ever dared hope at the same time because Jesus Christ lived and died in your place. The gospel (as Luther wrote) means we are simul justus et peccator—both sinful yet righteous" (*The Centrality of the Gospel*, unpublished paper).

"Through the person and work of Jesus Christ, God fully accomplishes salvation for us, rescuing us from judgment for sin into fellowship with him, and then restores the creation in which we can enjoy our new life together with him forever" (*The Gospel in all its Forms*, Leadershipjournal.net 2008 and Youtube: *What is the Gospel?* Tim Keller).

John Piper: "The heart of the gospel is the good news that Christ died for our sins and was raised from the dead. What makes this good news is that Christ's death accomplished a perfect righteousness before God and suffered a perfect condemnation from God, both of which are counted as ours through faith alone, so that we have eternal life with God in the new heavens and the new earth." (*Christianity Today*, 6/09) "The gospel of Christ is the good news that at the cost of his Son's life, God has done everything necessary to enthral us with what will make us eternally and ever-increasingly happy, namely, himself" (John Piper, *The Passion of The Christ*).

"The Gospel is the news that Jesus Christ, the Righteous One, died for our sins and rose again, eternally triumphant over all his enemies, so that there is now no condemnation for those who believe, but only everlasting joy" (Youtube video: *The Gospel in 6 Minutes*).

Tom Wood and Scott Thomas: "The Gospel Story is God's good news. Though I was alienated from God and under His condemnation, living a life full of doubt and disobedience, God loved me and gave himself for me (Christ died on a cross, paying my debt with God and rose alive from death), to forgive my doubt and disobedience; to be my righteousness and to be my power to believe God; to say yes to him in worship, no to sin and to get me home with great joy" (Thomas & Wood, *Gospel Coach*).

J.I. Packer: "The Gospel is a message about God. It tells us who he is, what his character is, what his standards are and what he requires of us, his creatures. It tells us that we owe our very existence to him…the gospel starts by teaching us that we, as creatures, are absolutely dependent on God, and that he as Creator, has an absolute claim on us. The gospel is a message about sin. It tells us how we have fallen short of God's standard; how we have become guilty, filthy and helpless in sin, and now stand under the wrath of God…the gospel is a message about Christ. Christ is the Son of God incarnate; Christ is the Lamb of God, who died for sin; Christ is the risen Lord; Christ is the perfect Savior…The gospel is a summons to faith and repentance. All who hear the gospel are summoned by God to repent and believe." (J.I. Packer, *Evangelism and the Sovereignty of God*).

Bob Heppe: "The Gospel is God's message of liberation: from guilt, alienation, and every bondage that hinders the human race from being fruitful for and reflecting the glory of God. The good news that Jesus preached is that He, as Lord of the cosmos, is now in the business of recapturing a run away planet. He came to destroy the works of the Devil—all of them, not merely the psychological one's that plague middle class people—and to bring the world under His saving authority. That means He came to reverse the effects of the fall, 'as far as the curse is found', by his life, death and resurrection" (*The Gospel, Sanctification & Mission*, unpublished paper).

Mark Driscoll: "What is the Gospel? The word gospel simply means "good news." The central message of the Bible is the gospel, or good news, about the person and work of Jesus Christ.

In 1 Corinthians 15:1-4, Paul provides the most succinct summary of the gospel: the man Jesus is also God, or Christ, and died on a cross in our place, paying the penalty for our sins; three days later He rose to conquer sin and death and give the gift of salvation to all who believe in Him alone for eternal life." (*Mars Hill* website and Youtube: *The Gospel, Mark Driscoll*).

David Nicholas: "The gospel is the good news of what God has done through Jesus the Messiah to make it possible for us to be forgiven our sins so that God can give us a new life and accept us into his family." (David Nicholas, *Whatever Happened To The Gospel?*) .

Bryan Chapell: "Gospel simply means 'good news.' The Bible uses the term to refer to the message that God has fulfilled his promise to send a Savior to rescue broken people, restore creation's glory, and rule over all with compassion and justice. That's why a good summary of the gospel is 'Christ Jesus came into the world to save sinners' (I Tim. 1:15). God's rescue, restoration, and rule apply to our spiritual condition but are not limited to spiritual realities. Through Jesus Christ, our God delivers his people from eternal consequences of human sin that have touched everything. Our salvation includes us, but it's also bigger than we are" (The Gospel Coalition, *What is the Gospel?*).

Matt Chandler: "If the gospel on the ground is the gospel at the micro level, the gospel in the air is the story at the macro level. Here we find a tour de force story of creation, fall, reconciliation, consummation —a grand display of God's glory in his overarching purposes of subjecting all things to the supremacy of Christ. As we examine the gospel in the air, we'll see from the scriptural testimony of Jesus's atoning work that the gospel is not just personal, but cosmic. When we consider the gospel from the air, the atoning work of Christ culminates and reveals to us the big picture of God's plan of restoration from the beginning of time to the end of time and the redemption of his creation. We may see the gospel extended this way in Jesus's declaration in Revelation 21:5, that he is "making all things new" (*The Explicit Gospel* and Youtube: Matt Chandler, *The Explicit Gospel*).

In small groups / triads (10 minutes)

Read Matthew 13:44-46

1. Why do you suppose we compromise our grand cause so much?

2. Do you agree or disagree that the ever-prevalent pursuit of the "American Dream" or being in the "inner ring" renders grace small and lifeless? Why?

3. In what ways are you similar to the lost people around you? How does that impact the way you talk to them about the Gospel?

4. Everyone has something or someone who takes his or her breath away. If the hidden treasure or pearl of great price doesn't do that for you, something else will. What is that 'something else' for you?

5. Review your "elevator" version. Are there any changes you would make? Do you need to make any additions or subtractions?

II. What is an "Evangelist"?

"In Christ, God was reconciling the world to himself, not counting their trespasses against them, and entrusting to us the message of reconciliation. Therefore, we are ambassadors for Christ, God making his appeal through us. We implore you on behalf of Christ, be reconciled to God. For our sake he made him to be sin who knew no sin, so that in him we might become the righteousness of God" (2 Cor. 5:19-21 ESV).

"We must be about peopling new churches with the un-churched. One way or another… our focus must be on bringing God's lost people into the kingdom. If a church is to expand God's kingdom, if its to be healthy…**then the leader should evidence and model evangelistic effectiveness**" (Kairos Self-Assessment Inventory).

"The evangelizer, motivated by the gospel, is able to make friendships easily, build trust and gather people. He has a well-developed skill in reading people's reactions and knows 'when' and 'how' to guide conversations to talk about issues of faith and substance with natural ease. He anticipates a person's objections to the gospel and handles these with grace. When appropriate, the evangelizer is able to present a sufficiently full outline of the gospel so that an awakened person can believe and trust Christ alone for salvation through faith in Christ" (Allen Thompson, International Church Planting Center).

A. An Evangelist is motivated by the Gospel.

"For Christ's love compels us, because we are convinced that one died for all, and therefore all died" **(2 Corinthians 5:14).**

"Christian evangelism is seen by many as proselytising or 'winning converts', a competition between the major religions of the world. Reaching others with the Gospel is not a contest; it is an expression of love. We speak to people with the words of Life. A Christian must tell others about Jesus just like an inventor must share a cure for a deadly disease. The means of evangelism, therefore, are important. Manipulation or emotional appeals might seem 'effective' looking at the number of responses, but such methods deny the truth of the Gospel and the compassion of the Gospel" (Harbor Church, San Diego).

↳ ACTION ITEM: PERSONAL ZEAL FOR THE GOSPEL
Self Exercise (3 minutes)

Read 2 Corinthians 5:14-15, 19b-20

1. How is your zeal for telling people about Jesus? Is it strong? Weak?

2. What demonstrable ways has your passion to tell others grown? Shrunk?

3. Which are you more passionate about: being an Evangelist or being a blogger?

B. An Evangelist possesses a strong desire to "win" lost people to Christ.

Evangelists see the broken world around them; men and women living in slavery to their addictions, apart from God, on a path to certain death and are moved by it. Like Jesus, *"When he saw the crowds, he had compassion on them, because they were harassed and helpless, like sheep without a shepherd"* (Matthew 9:36).

They sing, "Oh Lord, this world is falling apart, Dying for love from a broken heart, Here am I send me, though there's really not that much I can do, What I have seems so small, but I want to give it all to you" (Keith Green).

Like Paul, they say:

"To the Jews I became like a Jew, to win the Jews.
To those under the law I became like one under the law
(though I myself am not under the law), so as to win those under the law.
To those not having the law I became like one not having the law
(though I am not free from God's law but am under Christ's law),
so as to win those not having the law.
To the weak I became weak, to win the weak.
I have become all things to all men so that
by all possible means I might save some" **(I Cor. 9:20-22).**

C. An Evangelist asks God to give him the gift of Evangelism.

"God gave some to be… evangelists" (Ephesians 4:11).

Church Planting Evangelists realize that if they do not have a gift of evangelism, they want to have it so they can be used to see others come to saving faith. They will have other gifts, usually some type of apostolic and preaching gifts, but they want those gifts to be accompanied with the gift of evangelism. You might not presently have the gift of evangelism, but the missionary work of planting will be more effective if God's Spirit grants you this spiritual gift. God's calling is God's enabling.
"People with the gift of evangelism care passionately about lost people and have a strong desire to see them meet Jesus. They feel compassion for the lost and seek to earnestly understand their questions and doubts so that they can provide a compelling answer. An evangelist often prefers being with people in the culture rather than hanging out with Christians in the church" (Acts 29: The Resurgence).

D. God uses the Evangelist to "persuade" lost people to repent and believe the Gospel.

"As his custom was, Paul went into the synagogue, and on three Sabbath days he reasoned with them from the Scriptures, explaining and proving that the Christ had to suffer and rise from the dead. 'This Jesus I am proclaiming to you is the Christ, he said'" (Acts 17:1-3).

"After this, Paul left Athens and went to Corinth. There he met a Jew named Aquila, a native of Pontus, who had recently come from Italy with his wife Priscilla…Paul went to see them, and because he was a tentmaker as they were, he stayed and worked with them. Every Sabbath he reasoned in the synagogue, trying to persuade Jews and Greeks" (Acts 18:1-4).

Church Planting Evangelists work to persuade lost people to believe the Gospel. The word "persuade" (Peitho) means to induce one by words to believe or to make friends of, to win one's favor; it involves using words, not just your lifestyle or your character. Paul was a Church Planter and he went to each city and tried to get his hearers to believe the Gospel; The Story; the Good News of Jesus.

It is not enough for the Church Planting Evangelist to try to make friends and "show them" what a gospel life looks like. A Church Planting Evangelist uses words, in the power of the Holy Spirit to try to persuade people to come to faith in Christ. They are wonderful "apologists" for the resurrected Christ.

E. God brings about fruitfulness in their evangelism.

"But when they believed Philip as he proclaimed the good news of the kingdom of God and the name of Jesus Christ, they were baptized, both men and women. Simon himself believed and was baptized.... Then Philip began with that very passage of Scripture and told him the good news about Jesus. As they traveled along the road, they came to some water and the eunuch said, "Look, here is water. What can stand in the way of my being baptized?" And he gave orders to stop the chariot. Then both Philip and the eunuch went down into the water and Philip baptized him" (Acts 8:12, 35).

"They preached the gospel in that city and won a large number of disciples" (Acts 14:21).

"One of those listening was a woman from the city of Thyatira named Lydia, a dealer in purple cloth. She was a worshiper of God. The Lord opened her heart to respond to Paul's message. When she and the members of her household were

baptized, she invited us to her home… The jailer brought them into his house and set a meal before them; he was filled with joy because he had come to believe in God—he and his whole household" (Acts 16:15-16, 34).

"Then Paul left the synagogue and went next door to the house of Titius Justus, a worshiper of God. Crispus, the synagogue leader, and his entire household believed in the Lord; and many of the Corinthians who heard Paul believed and were baptized" (Acts 18:8).

Church Planting Evangelists are people God is using to see others come to saving faith. They are not simply people who are hanging out and befriending lost people—or having them in their home—as good and important as that is. God is pleased to use Church Planting Evangelists to see people believe in the Gospel, and be baptized, coming into the church community as disciples of Jesus.

F. An Evangelist is willing to "lay down" their lives to see lost people come to saving faith in Christ.

"I speak the truth in Christ—I am not lying, my conscience confirms it through the Holy Spirit— I have great sorrow and unceasing anguish in my heart. For I could wish that I myself were cursed and cut off from Christ for the sake of my people, those of my own race, the people of Israel" (Romans 9:1-4).

"To the Jews I became like a Jew, to win the Jews. To those under the law I became like one under the law (though I myself am not under the law), so as to win those under the law. To those not having the law I became like one not having the law (though I am not free from God's law but am under Christ's law), so as to win those not having the law. To the weak I became weak, to win the weak. I have become all things to all men so that by all possible means I might save some" (I Cor. 9:20-22).

Paul said if it were possible he'd give up his own salvation to see his countrymen come to salvation. He lists the salvation of others as his first reason for his willingness to relinquish his rights as a free man in Christ.

G. Evangelist have humble-boldness in "telling" people about Jesus Christ and inviting them to turn by faith to Him for salvation.

"Now, Lord, consider their threats and enable your servants to speak your word with great boldness. After they prayed, the place where they were meeting was shaken. And they were all filled with the Holy Spirit and spoke the word of God boldly" (Acts 4:29-31).

"On that day a great persecution broke out against the church in Jerusalem, and all except the apostles were scattered throughout Judea and Samaria… Those who had been scattered preached the word wherever they went. Philip went down to a city in Samaria and proclaimed the Messiah there" (Acts 8:4-5).

"But Paul shouted, "Don't harm yourself! We are all here!" The jailer called for lights, rushed in and fell trembling before Paul and Silas. [30] He then brought them out and asked, "Sirs, what must I do to be saved?" They replied, "Believe in the Lord Jesus, and you will be saved —you and your household" (Acts 16:28-31).

Church Planting Evangelists are people who are lovingly bold.

H. Out of love for Non-believers, Evangelists intentionally and regularly go to where non-believers live, work, and play in order to diagnose and expose their cultural, spiritual and personal idols, and engage them with Gospel of Christ.

"So that we can preach the gospel in the regions beyond you. For we do not want to boast about work already done in someone else's territory" (2 Corinthians 10:9).

"So he reasoned in the synagogue with both Jews and God-fearing Greeks, as well as in the marketplace day by day with those who happened to be there…Paul then stood up in the meeting of the Areopagus and said: "People of Athens! I see that in every way you are very religious. [23] For as I walked around and looked carefully at your objects of worship, I even found an altar with this inscription: TO AN UNKNOWN GOD. *So you are ignorant of the very thing you worship —and this is what I am going to proclaim to you"* (Acts 17:17-23).

"And as he reclined at table in his house, many tax collectors and sinners were reclining with Jesus and his disciples, for there were many who followed him. And the scribes of the Pharisees, when they saw that he was eating and drinking with sinners and tax collectors, said to his disciples, 'Why does he eat with tax collectors and sinners?' And when Jesus heard it he said to them, 'Those who are well have no need of a physician, but those who are sick. I came not to call the righteous but sinners'" (Mark 2:15-17).

"The Son of Man came eating and drinking and they say, 'Look at him! A glutton and a drunkard, a friend of tax collectors and sinners!' Yet wisdom is justified by her deeds." (Matthew 11:19).

Church Planting Evangelists are not thinking about planting a preaching station for themselves. They know they are "being sent" by God. They live with a profound sense of mission. They spend between 25-30% of their time with non-churched people. They are not afraid of going to places where un-churched people hang out. As a Church Planter, you generally don't have a church facility anyway. You have to go out and engage non-believers on their turf.

I. An Evangelists prays for open doors of opportunity to share the faith (Col. 4:2-4).

"Brothers and sisters, my heart's desire and prayer to God for the Israelites is that they may be saved" (Romans 10:1).

"And pray for us, too, that God may open a door for our message, so that we may proclaim the mystery of Christ" (Colossians 4:3).

Church Planting Evangelists ask God to save others. They also enlist the prayers of others to assist them in evangelizing others with the Gospel.

Praying for Effective Evangelism-—open doors of opportunity

A. Personal prayer is the starting point for the Evangelistic Process.

- Ask God for fruit in your evangelism
- Select a target group—have a prayer list of lost people
- Pray for specific relationships to develop

Using prayer in evangelism contacts:

1st contact—ask individual for permission to pray for them
2nd contact is for a meal—get a lunch/breakfast and learn about their life, hear their story. Ask for specific prayer need (crisis or healing, etc). Pray regularly for the person.
3rd contact—ask about their specific need mentioned-crisis. Tell them you will continue to pray.

B. Prayer for courage and boldness to speak to them about Christ.

C. Prayer Walk in your neighborhood or community.

D. Use Prayer Current's book, *Journey In Prayer: Seven Days of Prayer with Jesus.* With this book, you invite people to begin to pray to God before you ask them to believe in Jesus.

↪ ACTION ITEM: PRAYING FOR OTHERS
Self Exercise (3 minutes)

Write down the names of at least 3 people you know who need Jesus Christ and begin to pray regularly for their salvation and for your loving involvement in their life

1.

2.

3.

III. Doing the "Work of an Evangelist"

"But you, keep your head in all situations, endure hardship, <u>do the work of an evangelist</u>, discharge all the duties of your ministry" (2 Timothy 4:5).

Their lives are a gospel. It's not simply a job or title or role. They do the work as evangelists as a way of life. It might be for this season of life, but they are doing the work during this season.

Most church planting leaders suggest that the Church Planter should commit to a minimum of 50% of his work in the first year for creating evangelistic opportunities—whether in personal conversations, appointments or small group/large group studies or events.

In *Evangelism That Works*, author George Barna notes the following: "While the majority of senior pastors in growing churches <u>do not have</u> the spiritual gift of evangelism, without exception, every single one of them is passionate about evangelism. That passion carries over into everything they do. It motivates their churches to be evangelistically focused. They consistently find ways to make heroes out of the natural evangelists and gatherers in their congregations. And they work hard to communicate the gospel in relevant and compelling ways to the unbelievers who come to their Sunday services."

Loving Strategies:

1. <u>Build Bridges</u> by getting to know someone's story. Be an active listener. Earn trust.

   "The vast majority of un-churched people believe Christians hate them" (Dr. Jerram Barrs).

It must not be forced, but natural. What is their "plausibility structure"? A plausibility structure is "A structure of assumptions and practices which determine what beliefs are plausible and which are not" (Lesslie Newbigin, *The Gospel in a Pluralist Society*).

2. <u>Enter into a dialogue</u>. Where does your story have common experiences with theirs? Include in your story and shared experiences—"I have known guilt or shame too".

All around you are people who have spiritual questions and you have the spiritual experience and wisdom to offer them answers. Many people are open to good conversations about important and profound topics such as meaning, faith, hope, death, goodness, war, life after death, and God.

"An important aspect of gospelling is knowing how to relevantly apply Christianity to cultural and personal concerns. Let others know that Christianity is not some dreamed up fairy tale but a coherent worldview that holds up under scrutiny and has application to the daily issues of all people. Know the themes of relevance for your community" (Craig Brown).

Tell how Christ met you in that darkness or your own "fallenness".

A Story-based Approach Using Scripture: Often it is hard to transition from discussion around the Bible to actually looking into the Bible. Church Planter/Pastor Jim Moon recommends a transition using Luke 15 rather than the

"Roman Road". "Depending on the depth of trust and interaction, ask if they would read a parable Jesus wrote. Flip open your Bible (or laptop) and have them read the Parable of the Lost Sons in Luke 15.

After the story is complete, ask them: 'Where do you see yourself in the story? Why is that?' Then tailor the discussion appropriately to answer questions and objections. There are powerful pictures of God in Jesus' parable: God the Father, our lostness (two kinds), the shame of sin and the need for reconciliation and the gap where Jesus is the perfect Older Brother who paid the cost to reconcile a lost brother to His Father.

After discussion, ask: 'Where would you like to see yourself?' Often the story has a powerful effect in bringing to light the propositions of the gospel and leads to a person receiving Christ."

3. <u>Give a Gospel Summary</u>. When permission is given, move to a presentation of Christ, but the presentation should be connected to the story line they told.

Do-Done Summary:

"Difference between Christianity and religion. Religion consists of what people do to try and earn favor with God. Christianity consists of what has been done for you by Christ. All religions are spelled "D-O" because they tell us we have to perform to earn God's forgiveness, but Christianity is spelled "D-O-N-E" because God sent His Son, Jesus Christ, to live the life you should live, die on a cross to pay the debt you should pay for the wrongs you have done and came back to life to forgive you fully" (Bill Hybels, *Contagious Christian*).

Slavery-Freedom Summary: "We were built to live for God supremely, but instead we live for love, work, achievement, morality, politics or power to give us meaning, worth or value. Thus everyone is worshipping something…living for something. But all these things enslave us with guilt (if we fail to attain them) or anger (if they are blocked) or fear (if they are threatened) or drivenness (we must have them or we won't feel whole). Sin is worshipping anything but Jesus and the wages of sin is slavery. Freedom is when we live for whom/what we were made for…God, in Christ. He is the only one that does not enslave" (Tim Keller).

Sin-Salvation Summary: "Sin is us substituting ourselves for God, putting ourselves where only God deserves to be— in charge of our lives. Salvation is God substituting himself for us, putting himself where only we deserve to be—death on a cross" (John Stott, *The Cross of Christ*).

Apologetic of Shalom: Instead of telling people they are "sinners", hoping they understand us, we ask a simple question: Are things the way they ought to be? Any relatively honest thinking person will have to say, No, things are not the way they ought to be. This opens the door to ask why? And what is the solution?" (Cornelius Plantinga, *Not the Way its Supposed to Be: A Breviary of Sin*).

4. <u>Give them something to think about</u>. People need "spiritual friends".

- Gospel of John
- *Epic*, John Eldridge
- *Mere Christianity*, CS Lewis
- *Reason for God* or *The Prodigal God*, Tim Keller
- YouTube videos—send them links to watch on their own Podcasts from your sermons (if you explain Christianity and the gospel)
- Offer them a copy of the *Storybook Bible* or *Jesus Storybook*

Write in others that the group mentions:

5. <u>Follow up</u> with a thoughtful and appreciative communication rather than a single presentation: "I can't tell you how much I enjoyed our discussions. It is really great to have someone to talk about important things like faith, life, etc…" Do not get carried away by a sense of urgency. People make 'mini-decisions' on their way to faith in Christ.

Church Planter/Pastor Craig Brown suggests: "If I told you that dragons were attacking downtown this very moment, you probably would not do much more than chuckle. I would not get much reaction from you. Why not? Because you don't really believe in dragons and think, at best, that they are an interesting concept. This represents the shift in North American culture today. It is not so much that people have listened to and found Christianity lacking in truth or substance; it's that they immediately write it off as implausible. Commending Christ with humble-boldness demonstrates credibility. Instead of thinking in terms of "I'm a Christian and you should be too!" (which may well sound like "I believe in dragons and you should, too!"), lovingly help people see the holes in their own assumptions about the world, and show them how Christianity addresses these issues. It is not your job as a Christian to convince other people why you are right and they are wrong. It is your calling to commend Jesus and let his Spirit draw others to be his disciples."

6. <u>Clarify often in the dialogue</u>. People who are in the process of change need to stop and get their bearings. New terms and paradigms take time to absorb.

    a. Questions like, "So what you are saying is...?"

    b. It seems like you are unsure about...?"

    c. "Maybe I wasn't clear. May I try again?" Clarifiers in a conversation can help people organize new paradigm-shifting material. Questions provide "handles" in the disequilibrium they are experiencing.

7. <u>Ask people to accept the Gospel</u>! Without pressure or fear, simply ask them, "Would you like to receive this gift God offers you in the gospel?" Let the gospel do its work. It is the power of God to save. Put your confidence in the Gospel and don't be afraid to ask people to believe it.

Church Planter/Pastor Jim Moon, Jr., relates: "I've had more than one occasion where I've been in dialogue with someone, and it seemed like they were unsure about what to do next. So now toward the end of many evangelistic discussions, I ask what my friend Walter Henegar dubbed 'Umpire Evangelism Questions' (1) So do you consider yourself a sinner who justly deserves punishment from God for your sins? (2) Do you receive and rest on Jesus Christ as Son of God and Savior of sinners? "One self-proclaimed agnostic was so ready and yet seemed hesitant to receive Christ. So toward the end of our time I asked him those two umpire questions. He quietly said 'Yes' to both. I looked at him across the table there at IHOP and said, 'Chris, you are a Christian.' The stunned look on his face was eternally priceless. He said, 'I think I am.' He's a changed man and a leader in our church."

> ↪ ACTION ITEM: INTENTIONAL RELATIONSHIPS
> **Self Exercise (5 minutes)**

Go back to the three people you wrote down on page 173.

1. Where are you in the relational process with each one?

2. What common experiences do you share?

3. What possible gospel summary can you use with each one?

4. What resource (book or YouTube) would they be most open to?

"Effective Church Planters don't live scripted lives; rather they write a new script for how life can be lived. They apply this reality to the churches they start, as well. And such creativity attracts and interests others, especially those who have been unengaged by the church in the past" (David Jackson, *Planted: Starting Well, Growing Strong*).

Conclusion:

My friend David Jackson, who serves with the Baptist convention of Maryland and Delaware, wrote in his new book, Planted: Starting Well, Growing Strong:

"Effective church planting is about reaching the lost and unchurched with the Gospel of Jesus Christ. Ineffective church planting, which simply "moves sheep from one sheep pen to another" and is not focused on reaching the lost, is not really church planting at all. All legitimate church planting is evangelistic in nature and purpose. Some might see that as an over-exaggeration, but regardless, the point should remain clear: the best of church planting is focused on reaching the lost for Jesus."

I am certain that some of you after working through this module have reservations, disagreements, or plain old fashion objections. After 17 years of assessing potential Church Planters, I have found that the majority of the candidates do not practice any form of personal evangelism and hate being asked about this competency because they realize it as a weakness.

For most, we have over reacted to the "decisional regeneration" approach—trying to get people to pray a Jesus prayer. If that is what you think you heard, I hope you will lay down your objections and pray through this issue more than you have. We have not offered you a method to get people to "pray a prayer". Rather, it is a reminder that the gospel is power and we must allow the gospel to do it's work. That means, at the very least, that we expose lost people to the good news, with words and actions.

If you go into church planting with an aim to evangelize in such as a way as to "Make Disciples", baptizing them in the name of the Father and of the Son and of the Holy Spirit, and teaching them to obey everything Jesus commanded, you will likely grow a church. Converts (disciples) need a church and that is what you are baptizing them into, the visible church.

However, there is no guarantee that if you plant a church you will make disciples. In fact, if you begin as a gathering place for already churched people, disciple making might become simply a program. Be a gatherer of others who want to evangelize, empowering them to reach other lost people in their spheres of relationships. Your vision of the new church must be to have a community of believers, missionally engaged in the city.

34188290R00104

Made in the USA
San Bernardino, CA
21 May 2016